PRAYING
GOD'S PROMISES
for MY MARRIAGE

Jon Farrar

Tyndale House Publishers, Inc.
Wheaton, Illinois

Visit Tyndale's exciting Web site at www.tyndale.com

Praying God's Promises for My Marriage

Copyright © 2002 by Jon Farrar. All rights reserved.

Cover illustration by Julie Chen. Copyright © 2002 by Tyndale House Publishers. All rights reserved.

Designed by Julie Chen

Edited by Susan Taylor

Scripture quotations are taken from the *Holy Bible,* New Living Translation, copyright © 1996. Used by permission of Tyndale House Publishers, Inc., Wheaton, Illinois 60189. All rights reserved.

Library of Congress Cataloging-in-Publication Data

Farrar, Jon.
  Praying God's promises for my marriage / Jon Farrar.
    p. cm.
Includes indexes.
  ISBN 0-8423-5609-6
  1. Spouses—Prayer-books and devotions—English. 2. God—Promises—Prayer-books and devotions—English. I. Title.
BV4596.M3. F366 2002
242'.644—dc21   2002001058

Printed in the United States of America

08 07 06 05 04 03 02
7   6   5   4   3   2   1

FOR MY WIFE, ISABEL.

MAY GOD ALONE RECEIVE GLORY AND HONOR.

PART 1: PRAYING GOD'S PROMISES
FOR OUR RELATIONSHIP

PART 2: PRAYING GOD'S PROMISES FOR MY SPOUSE

PART 3: PRAYING GOD'S PROMISES
FOR OUR HOME

PART 4: PRAYING FOR GOD TO BE
AT THE CENTER OF OUR MARRIAGE

CONTENTS

A BOOK IS ALWAYS THE RESULT OF AMAZING TEAMWORK. I THANK GOD
FOR BRINGING TOGETHER A WONDERFUL, FUN-LOVING TEAM AT TYNDALE HOUSE
PUBLISHERS. THANK YOU, RON BEERS, CARLA MAYER, AND KEN PETERSEN,
FOR GIVING ME THE OPPORTUNITY TO MAKE THIS VISION A REALITY. THANK YOU,
SUE TAYLOR, DAVE HOOVER, TAMMY FAXEL, JULIE CHEN, AND DEAN RENNINGER,
FOR REFINING AND IMPROVING THE VISION.

I ALSO WANT TO THANK ALL THOSE INVOLVED IN PRODUCING AND SELLING
THIS BOOK—DONNA GAMM, TIM BENSEN, MICHAL MISCHNICK,
JANINE BOLLHOEFER, AND MANY OTHERS. FINALLY, I WANT TO RECOGNIZE
THE FAITHFUL ENCOURAGERS IN MY LIFE—DAVID, ANNE, AND ALLEN CALHOUN,
TIM AND SARAH FARRAR, AND WINSTON AND LIZA JOFFRION.

IT WAS MY PARENTS, ROBERT AND JOAN FARRAR, WHO FIRST CULTIVATED
IN ME A PASSION FOR PRAYER. AND MY BEAUTIFUL WIFE, ISABEL, HAS BEEN
BY MY SIDE EVERY STEP OF THE WAY. A SPECIAL THANKS TO YOU,
ISABEL, FOR GIVING ME THE TIME TO WRITE.

MY PRAYER IS THAT THIS BOOK WILL INSPIRE YOU, THE READER,
TO MAKE GOD THE CENTER OF YOUR MARRIAGE, JUST AS WRITING
PRAYING GOD'S PROMISES FOR MY MARRIAGE HAS INSPIRED ISABEL AND ME.
MAY GOD BLESS YOUR MARRIAGE.

What memory of your wedding day do you most cherish? Saying your vows before your friends and family? Laughing hand in hand at your wedding party? Putting on your wedding dress? Catching a glimpse of the passion in your spouse's eyes? Escaping to your honeymoon?

For many couples the love and passion of their wedding day spill over into the next several months. The newlyweds are captivated by each other's love. But over time the messiness of real life begins to creep into the daily routine. Work deadlines clamor for attention. Housework and yard work become boring and are never quite finished. Little by little, the passion may begin to fade.

Why Pray God's Promises?

If we don't continually rekindle the fires of passion by reminding our spouses daily of our love for them, we tend to slowly forget the passion we once shared.

The same tends to happen in our relationship with God. The passion and love we once had for him fades if we don't continually remind ourselves of what he has already given us and what he promises to do.

We tend to be very forgetful. When trouble strikes, we forget what the Bible says about God's willingness to help us (Psalm

50:15). When our resources—whether financial or emotional—wear thin, we first think of the enormous challenges ahead. We don't naturally turn to our all-powerful God for help (Matthew 6:31–33). When we start wondering what difference we're making in the world, we forget that God has a good plan for us (Romans 8:28). As the busyness of everyday life fills our days, we can easily forget God. That's why a book like this one is so useful. It reminds you on a daily basis of what God has promised to do for you.

God's Promises Are for You

Studying God's promises is just the start. If you only *know* and *understand* what God's promises are, you will have only intellectual knowledge. It won't affect your life in a profound way. You have to *believe* with your whole heart that God's promises in the Bible are *for you.* This is often difficult. Deep down we tend to think that God isn't really concerned about every one of our "little problems." We find it hard to believe that "the righteous face many troubles, but the Lord rescues them from each and every one" (Psalm 34:19). We don't truly believe that the God of the universe cares about our marriage, even though the Bible says that "the Lord witnessed the vows you and your wife made to each other on your wedding day when you were young" (Malachi 2:14) and "God has joined [both of you] together" (Matthew 19:6). God is concerned about your marriage and wants you to remain loyal to each other.

Often the question is not whether you *know* God's promises but whether you truly *believe* them. That's why you need to go the extra step and pray God's promises. When you pray the promises in the Bible, you do several things. First, you *acknowledge* the truths stated in Scripture. Second, you *proclaim* your wholehearted belief in those promises. Third, you *claim* those promises for your spouse, your marriage, and yourself. Finally, you *pray* that God will do what he has promised. Then you can know beyond a shadow of a doubt that God will fulfill his promises, for "all the Lord's promises prove true" (Psalm 18:30), and God is "faithful to [his] promises" (Psalm 71:22). If you come to God in prayer, you "can be confident that he will listen . . . whenever [you] ask him for anything in line with his will" (1 John 5:14).

God's Greatest Promise

God doesn't give his promises to just anyone. Many of his promises in Scripture are conditional. He promises to give blessings to the righteous, and in contrast, he withdraws his blessing from those who pursue evil (Proverbs 3:33). When you read God's Word, it's important to note the conditions that God places on each promise. For instance, in Malachi 3:10 God promises to bless the people of Israel: "'Bring all the tithes into the storehouse so there will be enough food in my Temple. If you do,' says the Lord Almighty, 'I will open the windows of heaven for you. I will pour out a blessing so great you won't have enough room to take it in! Try it! Let me prove it to you!'" Yet the fulfillment of that promise depended on whether the people believed in God and brought their tithes to him. Only then would God pour out his blessings on their lives.

But how can we claim God's promises in the Bible if so many of them have conditions? We can confidently claim them because of the greatest promise of all. God has promised to save those who believe in Jesus. He has promised to restore them to right standing before him (Isaiah 53:1-6, 10-12). All of God's other promises revolve around that one precious promise. When we are in right standing before God, we can claim all of his promises because we are his children, his holy people (1 Peter 2:9-10). God made the ultimate sacrifice so this could occur. He offered his only Son, Jesus Christ, to die on the cross for our sins (Romans 8:3). If we turn from our sins and believe in Jesus (John 3:16-18), we can be born again as God's children (Romans 8:15-17). Because of what Jesus did for us, we can confidently approach God in prayer, claiming his promises (Hebrews 4:14-16). When a believing husband and wife come together to pray God's promises, there's extraordinary power. Jesus is present with them and answers any request in accordance with his will (Matthew 18:19-20).

If your spouse is not a believer, you can be assured that your dedication to God and your prayers are making your marriage and home holy in God's sight (1 Corinthians 7:14). You can use this book to pray for your spouse and your marriage. God is listening to your prayers (1 John 5:14-15), and God is more powerful than any unbelief (Mark 9:24). Pray that God will place a desire in your spouse's heart to join you at the altar of prayer. No matter what happens, never give up praying to God, for he will answer (Psalm 17:6). Sometimes God answers in the most surprising ways—and in his own timing. When you are faithful in praying and studying God's Word, God will help you recognize the ways he is fulfilling his promises in your life. You will be able to say with the author of Psalm 119:65, "You have done many good things for me, Lord, just as you promised."

PART 1

PRAYING GOD'S PROMISES FOR OUR RELATIONSHIP

THINK back to when you and your spouse were dating. How did you act during those days? Did you worry about what to wear? Did you spend time thinking about how you would spend your time together? Did you spend hours choosing the perfect gift for Christmas or a birthday or some other special occasion? Did you write long letters to each other on the days you were apart? No matter what you did, you probably invested a lot of time and energy in the dating relationship. That's fairly easy to do when you are just getting to know each other. But it's rare to see that type of passion and commitment in older married couples. Other activities and responsibilities may have sapped their energy, and they tend to spend their time on other people instead of each other. But when we do see an older couple walking hand in hand on the beach, showing affection to each other, staring into each other's eyes, it's surprising. It's something we usually point out to those we're with. That couple's love lasted through the years because they worked at it. They put time and energy into cultivating passion and love in their marriage.

So many things in life work against building a strong marriage: time commitments at work, at church, with friends and relatives; financial pressures; personality conflicts. That's why it's so important to pray for your relationship and to claim

God's promises for your marriage. God doesn't want you and your spouse to be *just* married. He wants you to show faithful and dependable love to each other. He wants you to be completely loyal to your spouse. And he wants you to cultivate a growing and enduring relationship with each other and with him.

THE PROMISE
GOD MAKES TRUE LOVE ENDURE

Love is patient and kind. Love is not jealous or boastful or
proud or rude. Love does not demand its own way. Love is not
irritable, and it keeps no record of when it has been wronged.
It is never glad about injustice but rejoices whenever the truth
wins out. Love never gives up, never loses faith, is always
hopeful, and endures through every circumstance. Love will last
forever. . . . There are three things that will endure—faith, hope,
and love—and the greatest of these is love.

1 Corinthians 13:4-8, 13

W E all have a deep longing that something we do, something
we say, something we build will last forever. And when we begin
falling in love with that special someone, we naturally long that
our loving relationship will last forever. Even teenagers show
this deep yearning when they carve hearts on trees and put their
names inside them: Amy + Bob Forever. But as adults, we soon
learn that very few things last forever. Buildings deteriorate.
Businesses close. Words are forgotten. And relationships change
and drift apart. Yet there are a few things that last forever.
Those things that are connected to God will last for eternity.
That is why Paul in 1 Corinthians can confidently proclaim that
genuine love will last forever. God is love—and all love that
reflects Christlike love will last forever. When you show that

4

kind of love to your spouse, you can be certain that love will last throughout eternity. When you are patient with your spouse, when you show loving-kindness, when you don't demand your own way, that type of love will endure forever. God has promised it. As you plan your day, find ways to show Christlike, sacrificial love to your spouse. Ask your spouse what you can do to demonstrate that kind of genuine love in your marriage.

PRAYING GOD'S PROMISE

Dear Lord, you have promised that genuine Christlike love will last forever. Empower me to love my spouse with Christlike love. Help me to be patient, kind, and hopeful with my spouse. You promised genuine love would endure through every circumstance. Strengthen my heart to endure the difficult circumstances that will inevitably come in our marriage. Help me to show genuine love during those tough times.

GOD'S PROMISE TO YOU

- Genuine love will last forever.
- True love will endure every circumstance.

THE PROMISE
GOD ANSWERS OUR PRAYERS

[Jesus said,] "If two of you agree down here on earth concerning anything you ask, my Father in heaven will do it for you. For where two or three gather together because they are mine, I am there among them." Matthew 18:19-20

D o you remember the first time you gazed into your spouse's eyes, captivated by the love the two of you shared? Do you remember the times when you spent every hour you could spare together, walking and talking endlessly about everything? It doesn't matter whether you are still experiencing that passion in your marriage or that passion has begun to fade in the face of the demands of everyday life. That passion is a taste of the untapped potential of your marriage. Your marriage can be a tremendous source of power, joy, and comfort. Why? Because God, the source of all power, is in your marriage and has blessed it (Mark 10:8-9). God is pleased when husbands and wives genuinely love each other and remain faithful to each other. So how can our marriage relationship tap this power in our marriages? Jesus points out the way: "Where two or three gather together because they are mine, I am there among them" (Matthew 18:20). Those of us who have believing spouses shouldn't neglect the power of praying together. When a husband and wife pray together, Jesus promises to be present with them and answer the requests made in his name.

If your spouse is not a believer, don't give up on praying about your marriage or praying with others about your marriage. The Bible promises that you as the believer bring "holiness" to your home and marriage (1 Corinthians 7:14). You can be confident that God is listening to your prayers and is answering them (Psalm 116:1).

PRAYING GOD'S PROMISE

Dear God, you promise to answer the prayer of two or three believers gathered together. May my spouse and I become prayer partners. Help both of us to appreciate the importance of praying together. Answer our prayers according to your will as you promise in Scripture. You are present among those who gather together to worship and honor you. We want you to be present in our marriage. Help us to find time to pray together consistently.

GOD'S PROMISE TO YOU

- God will answer a believer's prayers.
- Jesus is present with those who gather together in his name.

THE PROMISE
GOD MAKES OUR LOVE MORE PERFECT

We know how much God loves us, and we have put our trust in him. God is love, and all who live in love live in God, and God lives in them. And as we live in God, our love grows more perfect.   1 John 4:16-17

OUR marriages should be a showcase for genuine love. The center of any marriage is the love each partner has for God and the love each one has for the other. This isn't the kind of love that focuses on satisfying your own needs. No, it's the kind of love that looks for opportunities to meet the other person's needs. You might express love to your spouse by cleaning the house or planning a romantic weekend retreat. It's the kind of love that looks for opportunities to affirm, to build up, and to serve. It's the kind of sacrificial, servantlike love that God demonstrated when he sent Jesus to this earth to die for you (1 John 4:9-12). That is why the apostle John described this love as growing and becoming more perfect. Genuine love isn't the lust portrayed in movies. Genuine love is something that God himself teaches. Genuine love is something that grows deeper year after year as you remain faithful to your spouse. When you demonstrate that type of love, it can't be contained in your marriage alone. That type of love overflows into the lives of those around you.

PRAYING GOD'S PROMISE

Dear God, you are love, and you love me perfectly. Point out to me the ways you show your love and care for me today and every day. Thank you for your love for me. You promise that as my spouse and I live in you, you will make our love more perfect, more complete. I pray that we may always live a life of love, empowered by your Spirit. Please increase my love for my spouse. Teach me to love more perfectly.

GOD'S PROMISE TO YOU

- God loves you.
- He lives in those who practice true love.
- He will make your love more complete as you live in him.

THE PROMISE
GOD WATCHES OVER US

You husbands must give honor to your wives. Treat her with understanding as you live together. . . . Be of one mind, full of sympathy toward each other, loving one another with tender hearts and humble minds. . . . The Scriptures say, "If you want a happy life and good days, keep your tongue from speaking evil, and keep your lips from telling lies. Turn away from evil and do good. Work hard at living in peace with others. The eyes of the Lord watch over those who do right, and his ears are open to their prayers."   1 Peter 3:7-12

GOD promises to listen to the prayers of those who are careful to treat others the right way. And if you're married, treating others right starts with your spouse. Sometimes those closest to us see us at our worst—when we let down our guard in the evenings, start speaking curtly, and express our frustration or annoyance in a way that can wound our loved ones. We need to find opportunities each day to lift up, build up, and honor our spouses. Does she need an encouraging word and a warm hug? Does he need a listening and sympathetic ear? Scripture encourages us to honor each other in marriage. We need to find little ways to do that every day. God promises that when we do what is right, he watches over us and listens to our prayers.

PRAYING GOD'S PROMISE

Dear Lord, you promise to hear and answer the prayers of those who do what is right, and that includes treating their spouses respectfully, with sympathy, honor, and understanding. Help me to treat my spouse with understanding and respect. Help me to honor my spouse. May you always listen to and answer my prayers. Oh God, you promise to watch over those who do what is right. You promise to bless those who turn from evil. Give me the wisdom to know right from wrong and to choose what is right. Help me to refrain from paying back evil for evil. May you always watch over me as you have promised.

GOD'S PROMISE TO YOU

- God hears and watches over those who do what is right.
- He blesses those who turn from evil.

THE PROMISE
GOD COMFORTS US

All praise to the God and Father of our Lord Jesus Christ. He is the source of every mercy and the God who comforts us. He comforts us in all our troubles so that we can comfort others. When others are troubled, we will be able to give them the same comfort God has given us. You can be sure that the more we suffer for Christ, the more God will shower us with his comfort through Christ.   2 Corinthians 1:3-5

LIFE is certainly full of troubles. We see well-laid plans thwarted and career goals blocked. Enemies slander us. Family members become sick. Our hopes and dreams begin to fade away. God doesn't promise to rid your life of troubles. But he does promise to strengthen you so that you can endure days of trouble and times of heartache (1 Peter 5:10). God may be using those times of trouble to build up you and your family and develop your character (Romans 5:3-5). The more trouble God allows to enter your life, the more comfort he will shower on you day after day. If you are experiencing difficult times now, take time to sit silently before God, letting him comfort you with his promises. Meditate on verses such as these: "God is our refuge and strength, always ready to help in times of trouble" (Psalm 46:1). "You [oh God] are my hiding place; you protect me from trou-ble"(Psalm 32:7). "When they call on me, I will answer; I will be with them in trouble. I will rescue them" (Psalm 91:15). If your spouse is experiencing difficulties, you can claim these Bible truths for him or her as well. Commit your troubles to God today and trust him wholeheartedly to provide the comfort and strength you both need.

PRAYING GOD'S PROMISE

Dear God, you are the source of all mercy. You promise to comfort us. Have mercy on us. Shower your comfort on us, for we're living for you. Your comfort, oh Lord, will help me to comfort others better. Help us to see how you are using troubles we're experiencing. Help me to know how I should comfort my spouse and others.

GOD'S PROMISE TO YOU

- God will comfort you when you suffer for him.
- He will give you the power to comfort others.

THE PROMISE
GOD PROVIDES

Taste and see that the Lord is good. Oh, the joys of those who trust in him! Let the Lord's people show him reverence, for those who honor him will have all they need. Even strong young lions sometimes go hungry, but those who trust in the Lord will never lack any good thing.   Psalm 34:8-10

G O D wants you to enjoy your marriage. He wants your life together to be rich, and he wants you to rejoice in him and in his gifts to you (Ecclesiastes 3:13). Temptations from this world may entice you with promises of happiness. But only those who trust in God will experience genuine joy. God invites you today: "Taste and see that the Lord is good." How can you experience this goodness from God? By trusting him with your life, your marriage, your entire future. God promises that those who trust and follow him will never lack any truly good thing; God will give them all they need. You and your spouse can claim these promises for your marriage and your family. God is good. He will take care of you, no matter what financial shape you may be in, no matter what difficulties you may be going through, no matter what emotional turmoil you may be experiencing. You can trust him completely. He won't abandon you in your deepest need. He wants you to experience lasting joy, not fleeting

14

happiness. In prayer today commit your worries to him. Express your trust in his good plan for you and your spouse.

PRAYING GOD'S PROMISE

Dear Lord, you promise to provide those who trust in you everything they need. We trust you to supply our needs. You promise that those who trust in you will never lack any good thing. Thank you for knowing our needs better than we do and taking care of us. Thank you for letting us enjoy your good gifts.

GOD'S PROMISE TO YOU

- God is good.
- He will supply the needs of those who trust in him.
- Those who trust in him will not lack any truly good thing.

THE PROMISE
GOD REWARDS CHRISTLIKE LOVE

You husbands must love your wives with the same love Christ showed the church. He gave up his life for her. . . . In the same way, husbands ought to love their wives as they love their own bodies. . . . As the Scriptures say, "A man leaves his father and mother and is joined to his wife, and the two are united into one." This is a great mystery, but it is an illustration of the way Christ and the church are one. So again I say, each man must love his wife as he loves himself, and the wife must respect her husband.   Ephesians 5:25, 28, 31-33

T HE wonderful and amazing truth is that marriage was created by God. It isn't a human custom that will disappear in time. No, it's something God himself established from the beginning of time and promises to protect. When you married, you pledged to love your spouse through times of prosperity and times of deprivation, through good times and bad times. God promises to honor that pledge and that type of faithful love. Why? Because the faithful love you shower on your spouse points to the faithful, sacrificial love that Jesus Christ demonstrated to the church. This is a deep and wonderful truth. This type of love doesn't focus on one's own pleasure, express itself only when it's convenient, or look for some type of payback. Instead, every day you need to do something specific that expresses your love, whether it's saying, "I love you" or taking out the trash or meeting at a romantic restaurant or doing the dishes or caring for a sick spouse. Christlike love is a dependable love, the type of love you can count on when things are going right—and when they're not. What can you do today to express your heartfelt love for your spouse?

PRAYING GOD'S PROMISE

Dear Lord God, you have created marriage so that a man and a woman may be united into one. You have honored marriage by making it a profound illustration of the unity Jesus and the church have. Thank you for creating marriage and bringing my spouse and me together. Thank you for supporting the unity of our marriage. Defend our marriage from those things that would break it apart. In Christ, you have shown us the love that should exist in our marriage. Help us to love each other with a Christlike love. You have loved us sacrificially. Help us to learn to love each other sacrificially.

GOD'S PROMISE TO YOU

- God unites marriage partners into one.
- A godly marriage illustrates Christ's unity with his church.

THE PROMISE
GOD FORGIVES

*Forgive us our sins, just as we have forgiven those who have
sinned against us. And don't let us yield to temptation, but
deliver us from the evil one. If you forgive those who sin
against you, your heavenly Father will forgive you.*

Matthew 6:12-14

T HE wounds that hurt the most are often the ones that those
closest to us inflict on us. Whether it's the betrayal of a best
friend or the cutting words of a brother or a sister, we feel the
pain of those words and actions much more deeply than other
wounds. The same is true in the marriage relationship. When
our spouse hurts us—or we hurt our spouse—with careless or
critical words, it *really* hurts. And it's difficult to forgive. Yet
forgiving our spouse when it's difficult helps us to truly learn to
forgive. The first step to true forgiveness is to communicate
with each other. Listen to each other's perspective. Together
identify the wrongs, and confess them to each other and to
God. Then don't hold back forgiveness; it is the lifeblood of any
relationship. When we forgive each other for the insults we've
suffered, for the wrongs we've experienced, that's when we can
experience God's forgiveness for the wrongs we have committed. God has promised to forgive the sins of those who don't
withhold forgiveness from others. The type of forgiveness God

gives us is the type of forgiveness we need to show to our spouses day after day (Matthew 18:21-22). Thank God for his forgiveness, and pray for the strength to forgive your spouse.

PRAYING GOD'S PROMISE

Dear Jesus, thank you for allowing us to come to you to confess our sins. Help me to always bring my sins and errors to you, confessing them and asking for forgiveness. Free me from continuing to sin against you. Thank you for the promise that God will forgive our sins. Help me to reflect your forgiving spirit to my spouse. And, Lord, please forgive my sins.

GOD'S PROMISE TO YOU

- If you forgive others, God will forgive you.

THE PROMISE
GOD GIVES THE GIFT OF TIME

There is a time for everything, a season for every activity
under heaven. . . . God has made everything beautiful for its
own time. He has planted eternity in the human heart, but even
so, people cannot see the whole scope of God's work from
beginning to end. So I concluded that there is nothing better for
people than to be happy and to enjoy themselves as long as
they can. And people should eat and drink and enjoy the fruits
of their labor, for these are gifts from God.

Ecclesiastes 3:1, 11-13

EVERYTHING has its own proper time and place. Often we cause
problems for ourselves when we don't follow the seasons of
time. Some people procrastinate when they are supposed to
work, while others attempt to stretch their work hours into the
night in order to accomplish more. In today's promise from the
Bible the author of Ecclesiastes states a simple yet profound
truth: "God has made everything beautiful for its own time."
It's cute to watch an infant play with her food, but it becomes
annoying when an older child does the same thing. The sooth-
ing tones of a piano are perfect for an evening concert, but
when those same sounds are blared deep into the night, they
become annoying. Each thing has its own time. The same is true
for work and play. Even though the responsibilities of married

life can make us incredibly busy, God doesn't intend for us to work all the time. We need to set aside time to simply enjoy each other's company, to continue to date each other, to pamper each other. God wants you to enjoy his good gifts to you—including each other.

PRAYING GOD'S PROMISE

Dear Lord, you have made everything beautiful for its own time. You have given me time to work and time to have fun. Help me to set aside time to enjoy my spouse, who is a wonderful gift from you. You are the provider of the food and drink in my home. You give me work to do. All of these things are gifts from you. Thank you for the fruits of my labor—my home and the food in my home. Keep me from being consumed with how much I have to do. Help me to find time each day to enjoy what you have given me.

GOD'S PROMISE TO YOU

- God makes everything beautiful for its own time.
- He has planted eternity in your heart.
- He allows you to enjoy the fruits of your labor.

THE PROMISE
GOD MAKES US ONE

The Lord God said, "It is not good for the man to be alone. I will make a companion who will help him." . . . So the Lord God caused Adam to fall into a deep sleep. He took one of Adam's ribs and closed up the place from which he had taken it. Then the Lord God made a woman from the rib and brought her to Adam. "At last!" Adam exclaimed. "She is part of my own flesh and bone! She will be called 'woman,' because she was taken out of a man." This explains why a man leaves his father and mother and is joined to his wife, and the two are united into one.   Genesis 2:18, 21-24

H A V E you experienced the gnawing feeling in your stomach that comes when you grow lonely, when you feel alone and abandoned by friends and family? Being alone isn't good for us, and God knows that. At the beginning of time, God refused to leave Adam alone. God knew that life was best experienced in a loving and caring relationship. He created Adam, as a human being, with the ability to experience a meaningful relationship with his Creator. That is why it wasn't good for Adam to be alone. Adam needed to experience a meaningful, intimate relationship with someone else to be complete. So God created both Adam and Eve, male and female, in his own image (Genesis 1:27). Together, in relationship, males and females reflect

God's image. Together, men and women united in marriage show what it means to love and serve, despite each other's differences. Certainly companionship that expresses God's love can be experienced outside of marriage, among genuine friends (Proverbs 17:17). But the Bible tells us that a loving marriage relationship reflects God's love in a unique way (Ephesians 5:31-32). Pray that you will be a loving companion to your spouse.

PRAYING GOD'S PROMISE

Dear God, you created marriage for our good. You didn't want us to be alone but to have a faithful and loving companion. Thank you for my spouse, my lifelong companion. Help me to be loving and supportive to my spouse. You promise to unite husband and wife into one. Do this in my marriage. Give us unity of heart and mind. May we always love and support each other in all that you have called us to do.

GOD'S PROMISE TO YOU

- God will make you and your spouse one.

THE PROMISE
GOD IS FAITHFUL

To the faithful you show yourself faithful; to those with integrity you show integrity. To the pure you show yourself pure, but to the wicked you show yourself hostile. You rescue those who are humble. . . . As for God, his way is perfect. All the Lord's promises prove true. He is a shield for all who look to him for protection. Psalm 18:25-27, 30

A hot morning shower. A fresh cup of coffee. The lights in your kitchen and bathroom. What would you do if you were deprived of the basics of your dependable morning routine? Many of us would start shutting down. It's easy to take hot water and electricity for granted. The same is true of *faithful love*. It's easy to take for granted the person who is always there to listen to your problems. It's easy to take for granted the person you run to when you're frustrated or in trouble. It's even easier to take for granted God's faithful care for you and your spouse. Every day God sustains the world in which we move and live. He provides food, clothing, and opportunities for employment. Most important, he showers love and concern on us every day. Our God is a faithful God. He is entirely dependable.

That same type of faithful and dependable love is the foundation of every strong marriage. Love is cheap if it's given only when things are going fine. Fickle love is worthless. We need love most when things aren't going well, when our lives are falling apart. In our marriages we need to be careful not to place conditions on our love. Our love for our spouses must be consistent and dependable. The morning greeting. The shared cup of coffee or evening dinner. The daily cuddle and evening kiss. What would you do without those daily reminders of your spouse's love?

PRAYING GOD'S PROMISE
Dear God, you promise to show yourself faithful to those who are faithful. I want to be faithful to you, God, and to my spouse and my family. Thank you for promising to shower your faithful love on my marriage. You promise to show yourself pure to those who are careful to be pure. Protect my heart and my life from evil. Cleanse my marriage and make it pure. You promise to protect those who call upon you, and so I call upon you. Please protect my marriage.

GOD'S PROMISE TO YOU
- God shows himself faithful to those who are faithful.
- He shows himself pure to those who are pure.
- He rescues the humble.
- He protects those who call upon him.

THE PROMISE
GOD FAVORS OUR MARRIAGE

The man who finds a wife finds a treasure and receives favor from the Lord.   Proverbs 18:22

W HAT'S the treasure in your life? Is it your career path? Is it your investment portfolio? Is it your home? Scripture speaks of our marriage and families, our spouse and children, as treasures and gifts from God (Psalm 127:3). Many of the things we're tempted to seek are transitory. Fame fades. Riches rot. Clothes wear away. It's the people in your life who are eternal. God has created their souls for eternity (Ecclesiastes 3:11). That's why Jesus described people giving up everything they owned in order to enter God's kingdom. True treasure that will never fade or disappear belongs to God alone. Every so often we need to check up on our priorities. Are we putting God first in our lives? Are we doing something every day to cultivate a loving relationship with our husband or wife? Those things are important because they last. Do you think of your spouse as a treasure? What one thing can you do today to demonstrate that you value your spouse?

PRAYING GOD'S PROMISE

Dear God, you promise to shower favor on our marriage and to bless it. Thank you for that promise. Bless and favor my marriage and family. Help me to appreciate my spouse as a wonderful treasure, an amazing gift from you. Thank you for bringing us together. Show me new ways of demonstrating my value for my spouse.

GOD'S PROMISE TO YOU

- God favors those who honor their marriage.

THE PROMISE
GOD GIVES SPECIAL ABILITIES

Be humble and gentle. Be patient with each other, making
allowance for each other's faults because of your love. Always
keep yourselves united in the Holy Spirit, and bind yourselves
together with peace. We are all one body, we have the same
Spirit, and we have all been called to the same glorious future.
There is only one Lord, one faith, one baptism, and there is
only one God and Father, who is over us all and in us all and
living through us all. However, he has given each one of us a
special gift according to the generosity of Christ.

Ephesians 4:2-7

DIFFERENCES often cause friction. An extremely focused person
may rub a more laid-back person the wrong way. A carefree
person who leaves things messy often irritates someone who is
neat and orderly. When we are annoyed by someone, we typically aren't able to see how much we need that person. A carefree wife can help a neat-freak husband to loosen up and relax.
A more focused husband can help a laid-back wife to become
more organized. The apostle Paul recognized that when different people work together, they need a lot of patience. Each
person needs to make allowances for the other. Each one needs
to learn to appreciate the unique qualities God has given the
other person. We need to look for the ways God is working

through someone who may annoy or irritate us. That is how we can cultivate peace in our relationships with others.

What special abilities does your spouse possess? How do those unique characteristics sometimes irritate you? How is God using those special abilities to help you and others? Ask God to help you learn to appreciate the ways you are different and to see them as gifts from God.

PRAYING GOD'S PROMISE

Dear Lord, I know you have given each person special abilities for a unique purpose. Help me to recognize and appreciate the special abilities you have given my spouse. Thank you for making me and my spouse the way we are for a purpose. Show us how we can complement each other as we serve you in our marriage. You promise to give every believer your Spirit and to call each person to the same glorious future. Thank you for planning a glorious future and eternal inheritance for my spouse and me. Thank you for giving us your Spirit to lead us in your ways. Help us to listen to your Spirit and to act as your children.

GOD'S PROMISE TO YOU

- God gives each person special gifts and abilities.
- He gives his Spirit to each believer.
- He calls each believer to the same glorious future.

THE PROMISE
GOD GIVES TRUE JOY TO THOSE WHO OBEY HIM

Remember this and keep it firmly in mind: The Lord is God both in heaven and on earth, and there is no other god! If you obey all the laws and commands that I will give you today, all will be well with you and your children. Then you will enjoy a long life in the land the Lord your God is giving you for all time.   Deuteronomy 4:39-40

WHEN Moses spoke the words recorded in this passage, he was very old, and the Israelites were ready to enter the Promised Land. Before he died, Moses wanted to remind the Israelites of everything their great God had done for them: the continual protection he had given them in the wilderness and the extraordinary miracles he had performed for them. But the most important thing Moses wanted the Israelites to remember, to keep "firmly in mind," was that the God of Israel is the only God and there is no other. Only he deserved the Israelite's obedience and worship. Along with this encouragement to remember, Moses gave the Israelites a wonderful promise: "If you obey all the laws and commands . . . all will be well with you." We who believe in Jesus can claim this promise given to the Israelites long ago. Scripture says "Happy are those who obey [God's] decrees and search for him with all their hearts" (Psalm 119:2). We can expect joy in our lives when we are careful to obey God because God is with us when we obey (Psalm 14:5). When we obey God, we grow wise (Proverbs 28:7). When we follow God wholeheartedly, we experience God's love for us because his Spirit lives within us (1 John 3:24).

Too often we're tempted to think that obedience sucks the joy out of life. Today's promise tells us that quite the opposite is true: Obedience leads to true and lasting joy.

PRAYING GOD'S PROMISE

Dear God, Scripture promises that you will be with those who obey you, and you will reward them. I want to obey you, oh God. Help me to learn about your perfect ways and help me to follow your commands. May you be with my family and me, as Scripture promises. Dear Lord, your Word promises that those who follow you wholeheartedly will enjoy life. Oh God, I want to follow you. Help my spouse and me to follow you with our hearts, minds, and wills. Grant us true joy in this life and the next.

GOD'S PROMISE TO YOU

- Those who obey God's commands will experience true joy.

THE PROMISE
GOD IS WITH THOSE WHO ENCOURAGE OTHERS

Rejoice. Change your ways. Encourage each other. Live in harmony and peace. Then the God of love and peace will be with you. 2 Corinthians 13:11

I T'S so easy to complain, isn't it? Life is always too difficult, too busy, and too demanding to really enjoy it. Although we rarely view complaining as a sin, the Bible describes it that way. God chastised the Israelites, who were traveling to the Promised Land, for complaining about their circumstances (Numbers 11:1). Why is complaining so bad? Because it communicates a profound lack of gratitude for what God has given us. That is why in today's promise the apostle Paul commands the Corinthians to rejoice. No matter what their situation, no matter how meager their resources or how vicious their enemies, the Corinthians were to rejoice in what God had given them. They were to spread their God-given joy by finding opportunities to encourage each other.

It's all too easy to get into the habit of complaining to your spouse at the end of the day. Make an effort to be an encourager to your spouse, to find joy in the life God has given you. God promises to be present in the home of those who encourage others, to be with the person who cultivates peace and harmony instead of discord. The next time you are tempted to complain,

32

stop and think about how God has blessed you, and then rejoice in his goodness.

PRAYING GOD'S PROMISE

Dear Lord, you promise to be with us when we endeavor to live in harmony and peace. Help me to do that with my spouse and with those closest to me. Make me an encourager in my marriage, my family, and my community. You are a God of love and peace. You want me to find joy in you. Help me to understand how wonderful you are—that you are the God of love, the God of peace, and the God of joy. I rejoice in all of your good gifts to my spouse and me in our marriage.

GOD'S PROMISE TO YOU

- God will be with those who encourage others.
- He will be with those who live in peace with others.

THE PROMISE
GOD GIVES US POWER

As we know Jesus better, his divine power gives us everything we need for living a godly life. He has called us to receive his own glory and goodness! And by that same mighty power, he has given us all of his rich and wonderful promises. He has promised that you will escape the decadence all around you caused by evil desires and that you will share in his divine nature. So make every effort to apply the benefits of these promises to your life.   2 Peter 1:3-5

If you're like most people, you've felt entirely powerless at one time or another. Maybe it was when you tried to keep a New Year's resolution or when you ran out of time on a difficult test or perhaps when your son or daughter started driving. One of the times people feel most helpless comes when they finally realize they can't break a nasty habit or let go of a favorite sin.

Have you ever seen the hopelessness in an addict's eyes? Sin can grip our hearts and minds like nothing else can and make us feel completely powerless. But God promises to free us from the power of sin, from the power of evil habits that destroy our marriages little by little. He promises to help us let go of the sins that stifle healthy relationships. He can empower us to live godly and pure lives and will help us to grow in self-control, patience, and genuine love. When your marriage seems to be whirling out of control, when you feel completely helpless, you can turn to God. He promises to give power to those who call on him.

PRAYING GOD'S PROMISE

Dear Jesus, you promise to give us all the power we need to lead godly lives. You have promised that we will escape the immorality of this world and receive your glory and goodness. Empower my spouse and me to live a godly and pure life. Help us to escape the downward pull of this world. Let us enjoy your goodness throughout our life together. You promise that those who know you better will grow in love. We want to know you better. Teach us from your Word. And help me to grow in genuine love for my spouse.

GOD'S PROMISE TO YOU

- God gives power to those who know him to live a godly life.
- He will empower you to escape the decadence of this life.
- He has called you to his glory and goodness.

THE PROMISE
GOD STANDS BESIDE US

The Lord himself watches over you! The Lord stands beside you as your protective shade. The sun will not hurt you by day, nor the moon at night. The Lord keeps you from all evil and preserves your life. The Lord keeps watch over you as you come and go, both now and forever. Psalm 121:5-8

EVERYONE knows how difficult it is for a mother to sleep when her baby is very sick. Every cough brings her to her baby's crib. Every time her baby wheezes, she is there to take the baby's temperature and to adjust the bedding. A mother tending to a baby doesn't get much sleep. Her night is filled with checking and double-checking, holding and cuddling. That is how the psalmist describes God's care for us. He is like a concerned parent who lovingly watches his sleeping children. He keeps a vigil over us as we come and go.

God is just as concerned about the health of your marriage as he is about the health of a child. In prayer today acknowledge your complete dependence on him. Ask him to stand beside you and your spouse, to watch over your marriage, and to protect your home from evil. This request isn't too big for God. It's exactly what he promises to all of his children. You don't have to worry because God is lovingly watching over you and your marriage.

PRAYING GOD'S PROMISE

Dear Lord, you promise to watch over us when we come and go. Thank you for your promise to watch over our marriage and to protect it. You promise to keep us from evil and to preserve our lives. Please do what you have promised for my spouse and me. Thank you for your loving and protective care of my marriage.

GOD'S PROMISE TO YOU

- God watches over you as you come and go.
- He will stand before you to protect you.
- He will keep you from evil and preserve your life.

THE PROMISE
GOD ACCEPTS US

May God, who gives this patience and encouragement, help you live in complete harmony with each other each with the attitude of Christ Jesus toward the other. Then all of you can join together with one voice, giving praise and glory to God, the Father of our Lord Jesus Christ. So accept each other just as Christ has accepted you; then God will be glorified.

Romans 15:5-7

ACCEPTANCE is easy when everything is going smoothly—when your spouse is showering you with love and kindness, when you're enjoying a great meal or time together. But what happens when one of you is upset or the house is a mess or the kids are sick or everyday demands threaten to douse the romantic spark in your relationship? Can you accept each other when one or both of you are not at your best? It's a difficult thing to do, but Jesus did it for us. When you were still rebelling against him, Jesus was willing to sacrifice himself so that God the Father could accept you as his own child. Jesus accepted and loved you even when you were still filthy because of your sin (Romans 5:6-8).

As a Christian, you are to show that same type of acceptance to others. And you need to start with those closest to you—your loved ones. When your patience runs out, when you're thoroughly discouraged, look to God for the patience you need and for encouraging words you can say to your spouse. Every relationship has difficulties, and while God doesn't promise to take those away, he does promise to provide patience, endurance, and encouragement when you look to him (Colossians 1:11). Only then will you be able to show your spouse the acceptance and love Christ first showed you.

PRAYING GOD'S PROMISE

Dear Lord Jesus, thank you for coming to this earth, not to please yourself but to sacrifice yourself on our behalf. Give me your Holy Spirit as you have promised so that I can find hope and encouragement in God's Word. Thank you for promising us the divine power to live in complete harmony. I pray that you will empower me to be patient and encouraging with my spouse and to work hard to cultivate harmony in our marriage relationship.

GOD'S PROMISE TO YOU

- God accepts you because of what Christ has done.
- The Bible offers you hope and encouragement.
- God will give you the power to be patient and encouraging as you look to him.

THE PROMISE
GOD LISTENS TO OUR PRAYERS

We can be confident that he will listen to us whenever we ask
him for anything in line with his will. And if we know he is
listening when we make our requests, we can be sure that he
will give us what we ask for.   1 John 5:14-15

G o d listens to us. What an amazing thought! The Creator of
the entire cosmos—the universe that contains so many stars we
cannot count them—wants to hear us. He takes time to listen to
us and talk with us. He promises to answer those who follow his
good ways (Psalm 116:1-2). Too often we treat our prayer life
too flippantly. We skip our daily prayer time. We crowd out our
time with God by trying to do too much. To our own detriment
we ignore the source of our power. No wonder we're too
exhausted when our spouse comes home. The solution isn't
simply writing our time with God in our daily planner in bold
ink followed by exclamation points. We need to rethink how we
view our prayer times. Do we see prayer as just one more thing
on our to-do list, or do we view our connection with God as a
power line to spiritual strength for each day? Do we view it as
unproductive "wasted time" or as precious time to renew and
refresh our souls?

First John 3:22 says that "we will receive whatever we request
because we obey him and do the things that please him." The

first step to claiming this promise for your marriage is to spend more time in prayer, both alone and together. If both of you are believers, ask your spouse today about claiming this promise for your marriage and about sharing a time of prayer. That time won't be wasted. Instead, it will permeate your entire marriage with the strength and help you both need.

PRAYING GOD'S PROMISE

Dear Lord, you promise to listen to us when we bring our requests to you. Thank you for listening to us now. Thank you for listening to our deepest concerns and for caring about the welfare of our marriage. You promise to give us whatever we ask for that is in line with your will. Help me to spend time in your Word so that I learn what your will is. Thank you for the assurance that you hear and answer our prayers. Help us to see the time spent in prayer as an investment in our marriage relationship. Keep us faithful in praying to you.

GOD'S PROMISE TO YOU

- God will listen to you and answer your prayers.
- He will grant your requests when they are in line with his will.

THE PROMISE
GOD GIVES PEACE

Since God chose you to be the holy people whom he loves, you
must clothe yourselves with tenderhearted mercy, kindness,
humility, gentleness, and patience. You must make allowance for
each other's faults and forgive the person who offends you.
Remember, the Lord forgave you, so you must forgive others.
And the most important piece of clothing you must wear is
love. Love is what binds us all together in perfect harmony.
And let the peace that comes from Christ rule in your hearts.
For as members of one body you are all called to live in peace.

Colossians 3:12-15

MAINTAINING peace in any relationship is very difficult. Each
one of us is a unique individual who interprets and views things
differently. Whether in relationships in the church, among
family and friends, or in our marriages, conflict is natural.
When conflict comes, we need to follow Christ's example by
showing love and forgiveness in difficult situations. God loved
us when we were still sinners in rebellion against him (Romans
5:8). We need to show that same type of love to others by being
kind, merciful, and patient.

We all have faults, so we need to be quick to overlook those
that appear in our marriage partner. We need to be vigilant
about forgiving each other, and we need to resolve conflicts

quickly so that they don't simmer and result in resentment toward each other (Ephesians 4:26). Cultivating a love that looks for and draws out the best in people preserves peace and harmony. If we seek to show that type of genuine love in our marriages, we will experience Christ's peace. Do you long for peace in your marriage? Ask Jesus to point out times when you have not been forgiving, areas where you need to be patient, and ways you can express genuine love to each other. That is how we have peace in our marriages—when we look for ways to love and forgive each other.

PRAYING GOD'S PROMISE

Dear God, you promise to love and forgive us, and you have called us as your holy people. Thank you for loving me enough to call me to be yours. Thank you for forgiving my sins. Help me to develop a Christlike love for my spouse. You promise to give us your peace if we live according to your good ways. I want to live for you, practicing a life of kindness, gentleness, humility, and patience. Help me to love my spouse genuinely. Send your peace into my heart, my life, and my marriage.

GOD'S PROMISE TO YOU

- God will give you peace when you show true love to others.
- He will love you and forgive you.

THE PROMISE
GOD DIRECTS US

Trust in the Lord with all your heart; do not depend on your own understanding. Seek his will in all you do, and he will direct your paths. Don't be impressed with your own wisdom. Instead, fear the Lord and turn your back on evil. Then you will gain renewed health and vitality.   Proverbs 3:5-8

O N E of the most dangerous pitfalls in life is the temptation to depend on our own understanding and wisdom. The older we get and the more successful we become, the more we're tempted to rely on ourselves instead of on God. The Bible warns us against this temptation to grow proud (Proverbs 21:4). We guard our hearts from this temptation by seeking God each day and spending time studying his Word. The Bible promises that if we seek God's will in all we do, he will quietly but surely direct our paths. As we give our choices, our lives, and our marriages to God, we won't have to worry anymore.

When have you tried to fix a situation all by yourself? Today as you pray, commit your spouse and marriage to God and his guidance, and trust him to sustain the vitality of your marriage.

PRAYING GOD'S PROMISE

Dear Lord, you promise to direct our paths if we seek your will in all we do. We trust in you alone. We depend on you alone, not on our own understanding. We want to seek your will instead of our own. Please direct all of our paths. You want us to turn from evil and to respect and fear you. We know you hold our future in your hands. We know you alone are our God, and we respect your power and love. We pray for renewed health and vitality in our marriage.

GOD'S PROMISE TO YOU

- God will direct the paths of those who seek him.

THE PROMISE
GOD HAS PAID FOR OUR SINS

The ransom [God] paid was not mere gold or silver. He paid for you with the precious lifeblood of Christ, the sinless, spotless Lamb of God. God chose him for this purpose long before the world began, but now in these final days, he was sent to the earth for all to see. And he did this for you. Through Christ you have come to trust in God. And because God raised Christ from the dead and gave him great glory, your faith and hope can be placed confidently in God. Now you can have sincere love for each other as brothers and sisters because you were cleansed from your sins when you accepted the truth of the Good News. So see to it that you really do love each other intensely with all your hearts.   1 Peter 1:18-22

EACH one of us makes sacrifices for something. Is it for a well-paid financial planning career? for a teaching career? for adventure and fame? for world travel? for "the good life"? All of us have secret dreams for our lives, and some of those dreams may even be from God.

But what if you were asked to give up your life so someone *else* could freely live the good life? What if that person was a criminal? That is what Jesus did for us. He obediently gave up his life for criminals. And we can count ourselves among them.

The Bible says that the actions of Jesus are the ultimate picture of true love. Christ's self-sacrificial love is what true love is.

Have you showed that type of love to your spouse? Have you given up something you really wanted in order to demonstrate your love for your marriage partner? In this passage Peter says that you *can* love that intensely because you have experienced Christ's love.

PRAYING GOD'S PROMISE

Dear Lord, you have paid for my sins with the precious blood of Jesus. You did this for me. Thank you for saving me from my sins. Thank you for sending Jesus to lead me to faith in you. Your Word promises that I can be confident when I place my faith and hope in you. I can be confident that I have been cleansed from my sins. We place our faith and hope in you alone. Please cleanse our marriage from sin. Help us to love each other from our hearts with a sincere and intense love.

GOD'S PROMISE TO YOU

- God paid for your sins with the blood of Jesus.
- When you place your faith and hope in him, he won't let you down.

THE PROMISE
GOD'S GIFTS ARE PERFECT

Whatever is good and perfect comes to us from God above, who created all heaven's lights. Unlike them, he never changes or casts shifting shadows. In his goodness he chose to make us his own children by giving us his true word. And we, out of all creation, became his choice possession. My dear brothers and sisters, be quick to listen, slow to speak, and slow to get angry. Your anger can never make things right in God's sight. So get rid of all the filth and evil in your lives, and humbly accept the message God has planted in your hearts, for it is strong enough to save your souls.   James 1:17-21

IT'S so easy to take good things for granted, isn't it? All too often the prosperity we enjoy today tempts us to take for granted the food on our table, the home that shelters us, the clothes we wear. We don't consciously think of these things as coming directly from the hand of God. Instead, we're inclined to think that we have a *right* to a certain standard of living. But the Bible tells us that every good and perfect thing we enjoy comes from our loving Creator. And the best gift God gave us is the life of his Son to take away our sins (2 Corinthians 9:15). The one gift we need above all others is salvation from death and eternal life in heaven. The gifts we receive in this world will break, decay, or wear out. But the gift of life in Christ will last

48

forever. We need to be careful to build our marriages on what will last. We need to readjust our vision and set our sights on eternity by humbly accepting what we read in God's Word. We need to remind ourselves that the best gift of all is that God made us his children, his choice possession. And the best promise of all is that God will save us (John 3:16-17).

PRAYING GOD'S PROMISE

Dear Lord, you chose to make us your children. You chose to give us your Word and make us your choice possession. Thank you for loving us so much. Thank you for your good and true Word. May we live according to what we read there. Your Word says that whatever is good and perfect comes from you. You sent your perfect Son to save us from sin and give us eternal life with you. Thank you for the good and perfect things you have placed in our marriage. Help us to continue to recognize these good gifts and to remember to thank you for them often.

GOD'S PROMISE TO YOU

- God's gifts are good and perfect.
- His Word is true and has power to save you.
- If you humbly accept God's Word, he will save you.

THE PROMISE
GOD'S WISDOM PROVIDES SECURITY

By wisdom the Lord founded the earth; by understanding he established the heavens. By his knowledge the deep fountains of the earth burst forth, and the clouds poured down rain. My child, don't lose sight of good planning and insight. Hang on to them, for they fill you with life and bring you honor and respect. They keep you safe on your way and keep your feet from stumbling. You can lie down without fear and enjoy pleasant dreams. You need not be afraid of disaster or the destruction that comes upon the wicked, for the Lord is your security. He will keep your foot from being caught in a trap.

Proverbs 3:19-26

EVERYTHING from a new watch to a new car has a manual. Most of us spent days with the manual for a computer with little success. A manual is a guide not only to how something operates but also to how it should be maintained. The Creator of this world—the One who founded the earth, established the heavens, and created the seasons—has given us a written manual to explain how this world works. That manual is the Bible. In it God reveals himself and his character. He points out the way we should go. He warns us of the places where we can stumble. And he communicates the great truths that will help us live effectively (2 Timothy 3:16). If we follow what God says in his Word,

God promises to keep us safe and secure. There won't be any need to be afraid because we will be obeying the directions of the world's Creator. He will protect us from all harm, just as he has promised. With your spouse, recommit your marriage and home to God. Ask him to be the security for your marriage and to guide you in his good ways.

PRAYING GOD'S PROMISE

Dear Creator, you promise to be our security. You founded this earth on wisdom. May we always seek your wisdom and knowledge as we make plans. Please be the security for our marriage. We're relying on you. You promise to keep us from falling into traps. Guide us with your wisdom, and keep our marriage safe and secure in you.

GOD'S PROMISE TO YOU

- God will be your security.
- He will keep you from falling into traps.

THE PROMISE
GOD HAS A GOOD PLAN

"I will come and do for you all the good things I have promised, and I will bring you home again. For I know the plans I have for you," says the Lord. "They are plans for good and not for disaster, to give you a future and a hope. In those days when you pray, I will listen. If you look for me in earnest, you will find me when you seek me. I will be found by you," says the Lord.   Jeremiah 29:10-14

T HIS message was delivered to the Israelites living in exile in Babylon. They had been forcibly uprooted from the Promised Land and taken far from their homes. They could no longer worship in the temple in Jerusalem, which lay in ruins. What were they to do? Jeremiah's answer was, "Build homes, and plan to stay. Plant gardens, and eat the food you produce. Marry, and have children" (Jeremiah 29:5-6). Were the exiles to give up on the possibility of living in the land God had promised their ancestors? In today's verses Jeremiah answers with a resounding no. God had good plans for them—plans that would open up their future and give them hope. Although the Israelites couldn't imagine being able to return to their homeland, God was working out his good plan to bring that about in his time.

The same God who had a good plan for the exiles has a good plan for you if you have placed your faith in Jesus. He is working out his good purposes for you (Romans 8:28). You may not be able to see the "goodness" that can come from your present difficulties, but God is working behind the scenes to orchestrate his good purposes in your life and in your marriage. Talk to God today in prayer. Ask him to fill your heart with hope and confidence in his good plan for your marriage.

PRAYING GOD'S PROMISE

Dear God, your Word promises that you have a very good plan for the future of those who love you. We love you, and we want to follow you. Help us to trust in your good purpose for our lives together. Guide my spouse and me along your perfect path. You have said that you will make yourself known to those who seek you. You will listen to those who pray to you. We are seeking you in all we do. Help us to find you and your perfect ways. We offer our prayers and requests to you. Listen to us and answer us, as you have promised you will.

GOD'S PROMISE TO YOU

- God has a good plan for his people.
- He will listen to those who pray to him.
- He will allow himself to be found by those who seek him.

THE PROMISE
GOD HONORS HUMBLE SERVANTS

Serve each other in humility, for "God sets himself against the proud, but he shows favor to the humble." So humble yourselves under the mighty power of God, and in his good time he will honor you. Give all your worries and cares to God, for he cares about what happens to you.   1 Peter 5:5-7

I T'S natural to want to be served. When we're eating at a restaurant, we expect good service. When we hire a plumber, we want quick and courteous service. Many of us are more used to being served than serving. But the Bible encourages us to serve each other in humility. This is especially important in marriages. If a husband and wife are putting their own interests above those of their spouse, a marriage can quickly fall apart. It's only when we serve our spouse first that we will create a loving and uplifting marriage partnership.

The world may encourage us to be proud and to demand a certain level of service, but the Bible promises that God will oppose the proud. So it's up to us to humble ourselves before God so that *he* can show us favor. Instead of looking out for our own interests, we need to let God look out for our interests. When we place our lives in God's hands, we can let go of our worries and cares because we know that God cares about what happens to us.

Take time to humble yourself before God today. Ask him to identify ways you can lovingly and humbly serve your spouse. Then pray for the strength and support to do his will.

PRAYING GOD'S PROMISE

Dear Lord, your Word promises that you show favor to the humble and honor them. We humble ourselves before you. You are strong, and we are weak. We look to you for strength and support in our struggles. Your Word promises that you care about what happens to us. Thank you for caring about our marriage. Help us to look for ways to serve each other and you in our marriage.

GOD'S PROMISE TO YOU

- God honors those who are humble.
- God cares what happens to you.

THE PROMISE
GOD BLESSES FAITHFUL PARTNERS

Let your wife be a fountain of blessing for you. Rejoice in the wife of your youth. She is a loving doe, a graceful deer. . . . May you always be captivated by her love. . . . For the Lord sees clearly what a man does, examining every path he takes. An evil man is held captive by his own sins; they are ropes that catch and hold him. He will die for lack of self-control; he will be lost because of his incredible folly.

Proverbs 5:18-19, 21-23

THE Bible makes it clear that God blesses those who honor their marriage vows. God created marriage in order to mirror the love he has for the church (Ephesians 5:31-32). That is why God hates it when people break or ignore their marriage vows (Malachi 2:16). God is pleased when our marriages show a self-sacrificing, dependable love—the type of love that doesn't throw someone away because the fires of passion have cooled. This is a picture of the faithful love that Jesus showers on the people of God (Ephesians 5:25-29). In today's promise from Scripture the author of Proverbs states this biblical truth succinctly for husbands: "Let your wife be a fountain of blessing for you. Rejoice in the wife of your youth." In other words, "share your love only with your wife" (Proverbs 5:15).

The Bible promises eternal life to those who follow God's

good ways, but it warns that those who seek sinful pleasures will die in their sins. Take hold of these Bible promises for your marriage. Recommit yourself to your spouse, for God promises blessing for those who honor marriage.

PRAYING GOD'S PROMISE

Dear Lord, you see clearly everything we do. Your Word promises blessing for those who honor the marriage covenant. Help me to honor the vows I made to my spouse. Guard my heart from being captivated by someone else's love. Help me to rejoice in my spouse now and for my entire life. You examine every path I take. Your Scriptures promise we can find joy in our marriage relationship when we remain faithful to each other. Help me to exercise self-control. Help me to rejoice in my spouse month after month and year after year. Help me to always love my spouse, no matter what life brings us.

GOD'S PROMISE TO YOU

- God sees every path you take.
- He wants you to continually rejoice in your spouse.

THE PROMISE
GOD INVITES US TO PRAY

My heart has heard you say, "Come and talk with me." And my heart responds, "Lord, I am coming." Do not hide yourself from me. Do not reject your servant in anger. You have always been my helper. Don't leave me now; don't abandon me, O God of my salvation! Even if my father and mother abandon me, the Lord will hold me close. . . . I am confident that I will see the Lord's goodness while I am here in the land of the living. Wait patiently for the Lord. Be brave and courageous. Yes, wait patiently for the Lord. Psalm 27:8-10, 13-14

"COME and talk with me." You might expect your spouse to invite you to talk over coffee on a Friday evening, but have you thought about how God has invited you to talk with him? Every day he invites you to come to him in prayer, to tell him your needs and worries and to give him your thanks and praise. Every Sunday he invites you to join with other believers in a discussion of God's greatness and a celebration of God himself. Meditate on the fact that the Creator of the universe invites you to talk with him. Every time you approach God in prayer, your heart should be filled with anticipation and wonder. God himself is listening to you! He is there, holding you close, never abandoning you in your time of need. You can be confident that God has a good plan for you and that he wants to show you his goodness (Psalm 31:19). So, like David, quiet your heart before God and wait on him. He controls the world, and he has a good plan for you because you are his child.

PRAYING GOD'S PROMISE

Dear God, you invite us to come and talk with you. Help us to take your invitation seriously. We want to have a relationship with you, our Creator. When everyday life distracts us, prompt us to come to you in prayer. Your Word promises that you will never abandon us, that you will hold us close. We wait patiently on you, oh God. We are confident that you will show your goodness to us. Thank you for promising never to abandon us.

GOD'S PROMISE TO YOU

- God invites you to talk with him.
- He will hold you close and never abandon you.

THE PROMISE
GOD STORES UP BLESSINGS FOR US

Your goodness is so great! You have stored up great blessings for those who honor you. You have done so much for those who come to you for protection, blessing them before the watching world. . . . Love the Lord, all you faithful ones! For the Lord protects those who are loyal to him, but he harshly punishes all who are arrogant. So be strong and take courage, all you who put your hope in the Lord! Psalm 31:19, 23-24

WHEN we enter someone's home, we can quickly determine what's important to the people who live there. If the husband enjoys golfing, there will be golf clubs in the corner and golf magazines on the coffee table. If the wife enjoys reading, there will be bookshelves throughout the home. We collect and store up things that are important to us. If family and friends are important to us, we have a large picture album. If security and money are important to us, we store up money in investment portfolios. The Bible encourages us to store up treasures in heaven (Matthew 6:19-21). We can certainly have interests and hobbies in this world, but we need to double-check where our first priority in life is. We need to rely on the storehouse of blessings God has for us instead of trying to store up things that will rust and fade away. We need to find our identity in God and his will for us instead of defining our identity with our possessions. God wants us to place our ultimate hope in him.

Where does your real allegiance lie? What direction is your marriage going? Are you and your spouse careful to store up treasures in heaven? Spend time evaluating your life and marriage and what your life says about your ultimate hope. Ask God to show you where you need to rethink your priorities.

PRAYING GOD'S PROMISE

Dear God, your Word promises that you will bless those who honor you. Thank you for being so good to us. You have promised that you bless those who come to you for protection and protect those who are loyal to you. We place our hope in you, oh God. We come to you for protection. Bless and protect our marriage as we honor you.

GOD'S PROMISE TO YOU

- God will bless those who honor him.
- He will protect those who are loyal to him.

THE PROMISE
GOD ESTABLISHES THE GODLY

The Lord approves of those who are good, but he condemns those who plan wickedness. Wickedness never brings stability; only the godly have deep roots. A worthy wife is her husband's joy and crown.   Proverbs 12:2-4

GOD is pleased when we find joy in his good gifts to us. That includes finding joy in our spouses. The author of Proverbs says that a worthy wife is her husband's joy, and certainly the opposite is just as true. A worthy husband brings his wife joy as well. The Bible tells us that those who follow God have deep roots. They don't have to worry about their future because it's in God's hands (Matthew 6:31-33). The roots of their household grow deep because they have consistently lived a life of integrity by following God's ways. Proverbs 12:2 tells us that the Lord approves of those who are good. God's approval on your marriage is the reason you can find genuine joy in your spouse and your marriage. Rededicate yourself and your marriage to God, to following his good ways. Acknowledge that any joy and happiness you have in your marriage is really a wonderful gift from God. Then find an opportunity today to express to God and your spouse the joy you have experienced in your marriage.

PRAYING GOD'S PROMISE

Dear Lord, your Word says that you approve of those who are good. Thank you for creating the marriage relationship for our enjoyment. Thank you for my spouse and for the joy our relationship gives us. I want to follow your good ways in my marriage. You promise to establish the roots of the godly. Strengthen and deepen the roots of our relationship so that we might grow closer to you and closer to each other. Help us to rejoice in your good gift to us.

GOD'S PROMISE TO YOU

- God approves of those who are good.
- He gives the godly deep roots.

PART 2

PRAYING GOD'S PROMISES FOR MY SPOUSE

M ANY of us don't realize how powerful praying for our spouses can be. When your spouse is overwhelmed, do you try *first* to give comfort or offer help? When your spouse is worried, do you try *first* to convince your spouse that there is no need to worry? When your spouse is angry or upset, do you try *first* to calm him or her down? Are your efforts always as successful as you'd like them to be? If not, it may be because you or your spouse needs to gain a different perspective on the problem. You need to hear God's perspective on the issue and be reminded of his promises.

Praying God's promises for your spouse can help you and your spouse to grow closer in several ways. First, your spouse may be touched by your concern. If you aren't praying together, you can tell him or her that you're praying about the situation or problem. If you are praying together, your spouse has the chance to hear your heartfelt concern as you bring the issue to God. Second, praying for your spouse can change your heart as well. When you commit problems to God in prayer, you can let go of the situation. God can help you to see the situation more clearly. You will grow less frustrated about the situation because you'll be reminded that God is completely in control. You can give the issue to him. Finally, praying for your spouse can make your marriage relationship more intimate. If your spouse agrees to join you in praying about the situation, both of you will draw closer to God together, and as you do that, you will draw closer to each other. You'll hear each other admit your weaknesses and fears to God and express your confidence in God. Together you can pray for patience and strength. Together you can pray for your marriage to grow deeper and your passion for each other to grow stronger. As you pray together, your lives and hearts will grow closer and your marriage will grow deeper and stronger.

THE PROMISE
GOD GIVES STRENGTH

I have learned how to get along happily whether I have much or little. I know how to live on almost nothing or with everything. I have learned the secret of living in every situation, whether it is with a full stomach or empty, with plenty or little. For I can do everything with the help of Christ who gives me the strength I need.   Philippians 4:11-13

STROLLING on a beach. Watching the sunset. Enjoying a friendly game in the park. What makes you happy? If we had our way, we would do what makes us happy all the time. But this life isn't like that. It is filled with challenges, difficulties, and troubles. Marriage relationships often suffer when we face daily challenges and emergencies. We may feel that we spend more time worrying about our lives than enjoying our lives together. What is the secret to dealing with this common challenge? The apostle Paul discusses the secret of happiness in today's verses. The secret for Paul was contentment with God's plan for his life. God had called him to a very difficult life. Paul faced persecution and trials of every kind, from ridicule to beatings to shipwreck to imprisonment.

The Bible doesn't promise any of us that we will have trouble-free lives. But it does promise that God will give us the strength to endure (2 Corinthians 12:8-10). The key to happiness isn't avoiding trouble in life. It is being content with the kind of life God has given us. It's focusing not on the challenges of our situation but on the strength God can provide. Is your spouse going through difficulties? Is your marriage suffering because of the extraordinary demands of everyday life? Commit those troubles to God, and ask God to empower you and your spouse as you look to him for strength.

PRAYING GOD'S PROMISE

Dear Lord Jesus, your Word promises that you will give us the strength we need. Give my spouse the strength he or she needs for today. Help both of us to learn to be content, whether we have little or much. Help us to focus on serving you. You promise to provide the power we need in order to endure difficult situations. We give you the difficulties and troubles of today, and we trust you to make your strength work in our weakness. Give us the power to endure our difficulties and the wisdom to see opportunities in every situation.

GOD'S PROMISE TO YOU

● God will give you the strength you need as you look to him.

THE PROMISE
GOD GRANTS FULLNESS OF LIFE

I pray that from [God's] glorious, unlimited resources he will give you mighty inner strength through his Holy Spirit. . . . May you experience the love of Christ, though it is so great you will never fully understand it. Then you will be filled with the fullness of life and power that comes from God. Now glory be to God! By his mighty power at work within us, he is able to accomplish infinitely more than we would ever dare to ask or hope.   Ephesians 3:16, 19-20

T o - d o lists. Deadlines. Packed schedules. Most couples have far more to do in a week than there are hours in which to do it. Do you and your spouse ever go for a full day without a coherent conversation? Do you find yourselves waving to each other as your paths take you in different directions day after day? When the apostle Paul speaks of God accomplishing "infinitely more than we would ever dare to ask or hope," he isn't talking about cramming more tasks into a twenty-four-hour day. He's talking about the *significance* of what you do by his power. God is able and willing to strengthen your inner spirit, mind, and body so that through him you can accomplish eternal things for his kingdom.

What are these eternal things? Lives changed for the better. Changed hearts focused on Christ. People dedicated to God, his Word, and his kingdom. In short, what will last forever is any person or thing connected to God. It takes a refocusing of our priorities to accomplish the *more* that God promises. It takes a willingness to dedicate our lives and our time to his eternal purposes and a willingness to follow God no matter what he calls us to do. As you do that, you will experience the fullness of life that God promises to give his people.

Do you or your spouse want the strength to accomplish more? First, take time out of the race of life to refocus on God. Take time to pray over your schedule and your spouse's schedule. Ask God to show you both what is really important.

PRAYING GOD'S PROMISE

Dear Lord, thank you for planting your Spirit in our hearts. Help us to follow the Spirit's guidance. You promise that you will give us mighty inner strength through your Holy Spirit. We need that inner strength. You promise to accomplish through us infinitely more than we dare to ask. Work within our hearts so that by your power we are able to accomplish infinitely more than we can imagine, just as you have promised.

GOD'S PROMISE TO YOU

- God's Spirit gives you inner strength.
- When you experience God's love, you will experience fullness of life.
- By God's power he will accomplish more through you than you could ever dare to ask or hope.

THE PROMISE
GOD GIVES US HOPE

Remember your promise to me, for it is my only hope. Your promise revives me; it comforts me in all my troubles. . . . Lord, you are mine! I promise to obey your words! With all my heart I want your blessings. Be merciful just as you promised. I pondered the direction of my life, and I turned to follow your statutes. Psalm 119:49-50, 57-59

WHAT makes weddings such happy occasions is the hope you can see in the couple's eyes. When they look at each other, they see their bright future together, loving each other day after day. What hopes did you cherish on your wedding day? What hopes do you have today? Do they revolve around the one hope every believer has—the confident hope of eternal life with God? One of the greatest sorrows we can experience in this life is unfulfilled dreams and abandoned hopes. But as believers we know that when we place our hope in God, we will never be disappointed because he will never fail us.

In today's verses from Psalm 119 the psalmist contemplated the direction of his life to make sure it lined up with God's Word. We need to do the same. Spend some time with your spouse thinking over the direction of your marriage. Pray that it lines up with God's Word. When it does, you can be confident with the psalmist that your hopes will be fulfilled, that God will bless your marriage, and that he will comfort you in your troubles just as he has promised.

PRAYING GOD'S PROMISE

Dear Lord, you are our only hope. You promise to comfort your children who are in trouble, and we are relying on that promise. You promise to be merciful to those who follow your statutes. We commit ourselves to obeying your words. With all our hearts, we want to seek your blessing, not the blessing of this world. Shower your mercy on our marriage.

GOD'S PROMISE TO YOU

- God comforts his followers who are in trouble.
- He will be merciful to those who call upon him.
- Those who obey God's words will be blessed.

THE PROMISE
GOD REWARDS HIS FOLLOWERS

How happy are those who fear the Lord—all who follow his ways! You will enjoy the fruit of your labor. How happy you will be! How rich your life! Your wife will be like a fruitful vine, flourishing within your home. . . . That is the Lord's reward for those who fear him. May the Lord continually bless you.   Psalm 128:1-5

G o d wants to reward and bless those who are careful to follow his ways. Scripture is filled with promises like those recorded in today's verses. God wants a holy people who will tell everyone else how perfect and loving he is. The problem is that too often his children wander from his good ways. We forget what God has said. We're tempted to follow the crowd instead of following God.

One way we can break that cycle is to meditate on promises like those in today's verses. God's ways aren't merely good and true. He promises to bless those who are careful to follow him. He promises happiness and joy (Psalm 84:12). He promises true peace. He promises stability and security: "Those who live in the shelter of the Most High will find rest in the shadow of the Almighty. . . . He alone is my refuge, my place of safety" (Psalm 91:1-2). When we're careful to know God's way and follow it, we can be confident about our future. God himself is ensuring and protecting it. Our work will reap fruits we can enjoy. Make a commitment today to focus your marriage and home around God's ways. Make a commitment to study and know his will for your life, and pray that your spouse will do the same.

PRAYING GOD'S PROMISE

Dear Lord, you promise to allow those who follow your ways to enjoy the fruits of their labor. We want to follow you. Bless our home. You promise to reward those who fear you. We respect and fear you, oh God. Teach us how to obey your Word, and please bless our marriage as you promise in the Bible.

GOD'S PROMISE TO YOU

- Those who follow God will enjoy the fruits of their labor.
- God will bless the home of those who fear him.
- He will reward those who fear him.

THE PROMISE
GOD WORKS THROUGH WEAKNESS

To keep me from getting puffed up, I was given a thorn in
my flesh, a messenger from Satan to torment me and keep me
from getting proud. Three different times I begged the Lord to
take it away. Each time he said, "My gracious favor is all
you need. My power works best in your weakness." So now
I am glad to boast about my weaknesses, so that the power
of Christ may work through me. Since I know it is all for
Christ's good, I am quite content with my weaknesses and
with insults, hardships, persecutions, and calamities. For when
I am weak, then I am strong.   2 Corinthians 12:7-10

THERE'S a difference between feeling tired and feeling weak. We
become tired after spending a full day hiking up a mountain.
Yet when we get to the top, our spirits soar as we survey the
magnificent view. It's a happy fatigue we feel because we've
accomplished what we set out to do. There's a different type of
fatigue as well. It's the weariness we feel when we're defeated,
when all of our efforts have amounted to nothing. That's weakness. It's the feeling we have when we realize that we're not
strong enough to meet the challenge.

Even the apostle Paul felt this type of weakness. His attempts
to get rid of his "thorn in the flesh" amounted to nothing. Yet
God spoke to him: "My gracious favor is all you need. My power

works best in your weakness." The same is true for us. You and your spouse probably have different weaknesses. And you probably know your spouse's weaknesses better than you do your own. But God's power is all that both of you need. In fact, God loves to work through our weaknesses because then it is obvious to us that the power is Christ's, not our own. Don't be afraid to claim God's promise in prayer. Ask him to work through your spouse's weaknesses and through yours, using them as opportunities to demonstrate his power in extraordinary ways.

PRAYING GOD'S PROMISE

Dear Lord, you promised Paul that your gracious favor was all he needed. We know that is true for us as well. You are all we need. Shower your gracious favor on our marriage. Sustain my spouse with your grace. You tell us that your power works best in our weakness. I want your power to work through my spouse and me. Help us to be content in times of hardship. Give each of us the power we need.

GOD'S PROMISE TO YOU

- God gives us his gracious favor when we are weak.
- You will have everything you need.

THE PROMISE
GOD SHOWS UNFAILING LOVE

I entrust my spirit into your hand. Rescue me, Lord, for you are
a faithful God. . . . I trust in the Lord. I am overcome with joy
because of your unfailing love, for you have seen my troubles,
and you care about the anguish of my soul. You have not
handed me over to my enemy but have set me in a safe place.

Psalm 31:5-8

In Psalm 31, from which today's verses are taken, David
describes enemies who scorn him, neighbors who despise him,
and even friends who have abandoned him. He is in trouble.
Have you ever felt like that? Have you been in a situation where
even your friends are afraid to come near you? When that
happens, most of us feel utterly alone and abandoned. David
felt the same way. But he didn't let his soul become paralyzed.
He concentrated on the freeing truth that God was with him.
Although others had abandoned him, God had not. He saw
David's trouble. He knew David's anguish intimately. And he
cared enough to rescue David and set him in a safe place. God is
willing to do the same for you and your spouse. He enjoys
showing love when no one else will, and he loves to rescue in
miraculous ways: "I will rescue those who love me. I will protect
those who trust in my name. When they call on me, I will
answer; I will be with them in trouble. I will rescue them and

honor them" (Psalm 91:14-15). Do you or your spouse need extraordinary love to mend a broken heart? Do you need a faithful God in a trying and difficult time? Reach out to the God who loves to love. Call upon the one who knows your anguish. In the midst of difficulties you and your spouse can find joy, as David did, in God's extraordinary love.

PRAYING GOD'S PROMISE

Dear Lord, your Word promises that you are a faithful God who shows unfailing love to those who call on you. We call on you, oh God, when we're experiencing trouble. You have shown your unfailing love to my spouse and me in the past. Rescue us again. You see the troubles of those who trust in you. You care about our inner anguish. I trust you with all my heart. I know you care about my pain. Set my spouse and me in a safe place. Protect us from the people and things that can destroy us.

GOD'S PROMISE TO YOU

- God is faithful.
- Those who trust in him will experience his unfailing love.
- He sees your troubles and cares about your inner anguish.

THE PROMISE
GOD DEVELOPS CHARACTER IN US

We can rejoice . . . when we run into problems and trials,
for we know that they are good for us—they help us learn to
endure. And endurance develops strength of character in us,
and character strengthens our confident expectation of salvation.
And this expectation will not disappoint us. For we know how
dearly God loves us, because he has given us the Holy Spirit
to fill our hearts with his love. Romans 5:3-5

T H E best teacher is the one who pushes his students. The best
parents are those who see the potential in their children and
seek to help them develop that potential. God does the same
thing with us. He knows our potential. He knows perfectly and
intimately what we can be, and he wants the best for us. That is
why God allows problems and trials to come into our lives and
marriages. He knows these things will strengthen us. They will
teach us to turn to him for help and to place our hope in him
alone.

In the book of Romans the apostle Paul tells us that as believers we have been fully equipped for the problems that life offers.
Jesus has made us right in God's sight. We have the privilege of
standing before God as his children. We have the Holy Spirit,
who has filled us with Christlike love. And we can look forward
to sharing God's glory in the next life. So when we experience

difficulties and trials, we need to remind ourselves of these things. God has fully equipped us. He wants the best for us. And he can use any difficulty or trial for our good (Romans 8:28). If you or your spouse are facing a difficulty, bring it to God. Ask him for the insight and strength to handle it with grace. He promises to provide the strength you and your spouse will need.

PRAYING GOD'S PROMISE

Dear Lord, you promise to allow us to share in your glory in the future. Your Word says that problems and trials will develop character in us. Thank you, Jesus, for making us right in God's sight. Thank you for giving me the hope of a glorious future with you. Develop our character the way you see fit. You promise to fulfill our confident expectation of salvation. As we face difficulties, help us to learn endurance, to gain strength of character and confident hope in you. I know that you love my spouse and want the best for our marriage. Help us to be faithful as you work your best in us.

GOD'S PROMISE TO YOU

- God accepts you because of what Jesus did for you.
- The Holy Spirit will fill your hearts with love.
- God allows difficulties in order to shape your character.

THE PROMISE
GOD ANSWERS OUR REQUESTS

[Jesus said,] "You can go directly to the Father and ask him,
and he will grant your request because you use my name. You
haven't done this before. Ask, using my name, and you will
receive, and you will have abundant joy. . . . "The Father
himself loves you dearly because you love me and believe that
I came from God. . . . I have told you all this so that you
may have peace in me. Here on earth you will have many
trials and sorrows. But take heart, because I have overcome
the world."   John 16:23-27, 33

"A s k . . . and you will receive." What a promise!

Why do we so often ignore or forget God's promises concerning prayer? One reason may be that we have never experienced
anything like it. It's rare for someone to give something without
strings attached. It's rare for someone to offer so much without
expecting something in return. That's not how this world
works. But that's how God works. Jesus offers a free invitation
to everyone: "Come to me, all of you who are weary and carry
heavy burdens, and I will give you rest" (Matthew 11:28). In
other words, if you will turn away from your own ways and
come to him, he will rescue you and give you eternal life. What
an invitation! Unfortunately, our pride gets in the way of our
asking. We either want to go our own way or we want to play a

part in gaining our salvation. We want to somehow earn what we receive. We don't want to admit that we can come to God only as beggars with empty, open hands. We can't give God anything but hearts that are broken over our sin.

The invitation stands. Jesus says, "Ask in my name, and you will receive." Will you ask for yourself, your spouse, and for your marriage?

PRAYING GOD'S PROMISE

Oh Lord, your Word tells us that you love us dearly. You promise that we can come directly to you with our requests and that you will answer us. Thank you for loving us. It is amazing that you do. Please listen to us, and answer my requests for my spouse. Let us experience the joy of seeing our prayers answered. You have promised that we can have peace because you have already overcome the world. May your peace rule in our hearts as we truly believe that you have overcome this world.

GOD'S PROMISE TO YOU

- God loves you dearly because you believe in Jesus.
- He will answer your prayers when you ask in the name of Jesus.
- He will grant you peace and abundant joy.

THE PROMISE
GOD PROTECTS US

The Lord is my light and my salvation—so why should I be afraid? The Lord protects me from danger—so why should I tremble? When evil people come to destroy me, when my enemies and foes attack me, they will stumble and fall. Though a mighty army surrounds me, my heart will know no fear. Even if they attack me, I remain confident.   Psalm 27:1-3

T HERE is no end to worry once you start thinking of everything that could go wrong. Life is full of danger—from a collapse in the stock market to a car accident. Centuries ago David wasn't a stranger to danger. Enemies accused him of things he hadn't done: "Do not let me fall into their hands. For they accuse me of things I've never done and breathe out violence against me" (Psalm 27:12). They even hunted him down, and armies surrounded him, but he remained confident. Why could he do that? Because he trusted that God would protect him. He knew that the all-powerful Creator of the universe would come to his rescue. God would provide the light to illumine the path to safety. What army of trouble has surrounded you and your spouse? Follow David's example, and commit that army to God. Trust him to show you and your spouse the way to handle the situation. Ask God to rescue you. Then you'll be able to say with David, "I remain confident," because your confidence is in the almighty God.

PRAYING GOD'S PROMISE

Oh Lord, you promise to be our salvation and light. If I truly believe that, what reason do I have to be fearful? You will rescue my spouse from every danger. You will guide my spouse with your true light. Your Word promises that you will protect us. Keep me from being afraid as I trust in your great power. You are powerful enough to protect us even if we are surrounded by enemies. Thank you for the peace and comfort your mighty power gives us.

GOD'S PROMISE TO YOU

- God is your light and salvation.
- When enemies surround you, you can remain confident because of God's mighty power.

THE PROMISE
GOD HEARS THE PRAYERS OF THOSE
WHO SUFFER

Are any among you suffering? They should keep on praying
about it. And those who have reason to be thankful should
continually sing praises to the Lord. Are any among you sick?
They should call for the elders of the church and have them
pray over them, anointing them with oil in the name of the
Lord. And their prayer offered in faith will heal the sick, and
the Lord will make them well. And anyone who has committed
sins will be forgiven. Confess your sins to each other and pray
for each other so that you may be healed. The earnest prayer of
a righteous person has great power and wonderful results.

James 5:13-16

P s a l m 116:2 says, "Because [God] bends down and listens, I
will pray as long as I have breath!" Prayer changes things. In
response to a mother's faithful prayers God can change the
hard heart of a rebellious teen. Whether it's a prayer for
strength to handle a toddler or for strength to fight cancer, God
listens to it. Not only does God listen, he also answers. He gives
us strength to endure hardship. He graciously grants months,
years, and decades of life to the sick.

James knew the power of prayer, and his words in today's
verses tell all of us to be persistent in prayer. If you or your

spouse is suffering at this point, James encourages you to keep on praying. Certainly you should offer thanks for what God has given you. But don't be afraid to pray for relief from suffering. If you or your spouse is sick, pray about it. And don't forget to ask others in your church to pray for you as well.

Bring all of your requests to God. God loves to hear his children call upon him and then look for him to act. He loves to answer the prayers of those who follow him whole-heartedly. What a privilege it is to pray to the One who promises to hear and answer (Psalm 91:15).

PRAYING GOD'S PROMISE

Dear Lord, you promise to answer the prayer offered in faith. We believe in you. Strengthen our faith in you. Answer our prayers for healing, just as your Word promises. Your Word promises that the prayer of a righteous person will have wonderful results. We want to lead righteous lives. Help us to follow your commands. Strengthen our prayer life. May we see wonderful results from our prayers.

GOD'S PROMISE TO YOU

- God will answer the prayers of the righteous.
- Those who confess their sins will be healed.

THE PROMISE
GOD GIVES WISDOM

If you need wisdom—if you want to know what God wants you to do—ask him, and he will gladly tell you. He will not resent your asking. But when you ask him, be sure that you really expect him to answer, for a doubtful mind is as unsettled as a wave of the sea that is driven and tossed by the wind.

James 1:5-6

In every phase of our lives we can expect to face difficult choices: Should I accept this job opportunity? Should we move? How should I serve God, and within which church community should I serve him? How should we handle our current financial stress?

Making difficult choices requires more than mere human wisdom, so the first thing we need to do when faced with a difficult decision is to ask God for his wisdom. That's what James tells us to do in today's verses. If we come to God in faith, confidently expecting an answer, God promises to give us one.

Sometimes God's answer comes through the counsel of friends or church members, for the Bible tells us to seek advice from those who are wise (Proverbs 13:14). Sometimes God speaks through the Bible to show us his good ways (2 Timothy 3:16). At still other times God gently directs us through our circumstances. In any case, when you as a couple commit a decision to God in prayer, both of you should look for and expect an answer. God wants to guide your marriage according to his good plan (Psalm 32:8). He wants to be part of your decision-making process. He wants you to commit your plans to him (Proverbs 16:3). What decisions are you and your spouse facing at this point in your life? Set aside time to pray together for wisdom. You can be certain that God will answer your prayer.

PRAYING GOD'S PROMISE

Dear Lord, you promise to answer those who call on you with full confidence that you will answer, and so we call on you. We will do what you tell us to do. Answer our prayers, as your Word promises you will. Your Word says that you are glad to tell us what you want us to do. We want you to give us wisdom. Grant my spouse and me your wisdom for the decisions we face today. Help us to follow your good plan for us.

GOD'S PROMISE TO YOU

- God will gladly give wisdom to those who ask him for it.
- God will tell you what he wants you to do.

THE PROMISE
GOD'S LOVE EXPELS FEAR

We know how much God loves us, and we have put our trust in him. God is love, and all who live in love live in God, and God lives in them. As we live in God, our love grows more perfect. So we will not be afraid on the day of judgment, but we can face him with confidence because we are like Christ here in this world. Such love has no fear because perfect love expels all fear. . . . We love each other as a result of his loving us first.   1 John 4:16-19

T HIS world is full of surprises. Could you have guessed when you were a teenager what you would be doing now? Could you have guessed where you would be living and with whom? Often there are U-turns and detours on the highway of life. There are unexpected pit stops or obstacles along the way. The unexpected often causes fear. When we're not certain how we'll get through a situation or which way to go, we grow afraid. But the Bible tells us that as children of God we have nothing to fear (Psalm 49:5). God is in control of our future. Most important, God has secured our future for eternity. We don't have to fear what will happen after death, for the God of life has granted us an eternal home (John 6:40). We don't have to fear judgment, because the Judge of the world has made us right with him (Romans 5:21). When the God of love lives in us, we really do have nothing to fear.

90

What are you afraid of today? Commit the fears you may have concerning your spouse or your life to God. Remind yourself of the deep love God has for you and your spouse. Pray that God will help you to trust in his loving care and his good plan for you and your spouse.

PRAYING GOD'S PROMISE

Oh God of love, you loved us first. Your Word promises that you will cultivate perfect love in those who live in you. Make our love for each other more perfect as you live in us. You are a God of perfect love. You have promised that perfect love expels all fear. We admit that sometimes we're afraid. Grow a more perfect love for you in my spouse and me. And as you do, please expel all fear from our hearts.

GOD'S PROMISE TO YOU

- God loved us before we loved him.
- His perfect love will expel all fear.

THE PROMISE
GOD GIVES JOY

> I prayed to the Lord, and he answered me, freeing me from all my fears. Those who look to him for help will be radiant with joy; no shadow of shame will darken their faces. I cried out to the Lord in my suffering, and he heard me. He set me free from all my fears. For the angel of the Lord guards all who fear him, and he rescues them. Psalm 34:4-7

D o you enjoy watching the televised Olympic games? If you do, you know that the joy the winners of an Olympic event experience is contagious. That's one reason millions of people watch the Olympics so religiously. It's not simply to see the drama of the event and the excellence and form of the athletes. It's also to share in the contagious joy of the winners. In Psalm 34 David describes the same type of joy radiating from believers. All those who look to God for help will experience a joy so intense that other people can see it in their faces. David says the reason for that joy is that God has heard and answered our prayers. Our shame has been taken away. We have been set free from all our fears because the angel of the Lord encamps around us. He guards his people. Pray today that the angel of the Lord will set up camp around your marriage. Commit your fears and worries to God, and ask him to guard you and your spouse. He can set you free from your fears and grant you radiant joy as you look to him for help.

PRAYING GOD'S PROMISE

Dear Lord, your Word promises that as we look to you for help, you will free us from all our fears and will answer our prayers. We're looking to you for help. Dispel our fears and fill us with joy. We trust you to hear and answer us. We have read that the angel of the Lord guards those who fear you. We respect and fear you. Send the angel of the Lord to guard my spouse and me and to make us radiant with the joy that comes only from looking to you for our help.

GOD'S PROMISE TO YOU

- God hears and answers your prayers when you ask him for help.
- He gives you joy.
- He is able to set you free from your fears.

THE PROMISE
GOD LIFTS UP THE BURDENED

The Lord is faithful in all he says; he is gracious in all he does. The Lord helps the fallen and lifts up those bent beneath their loads. All eyes look to you for help; you give them their food as they need it. When you open your hand, you satisfy the hunger and thirst of every living thing.   Psalm 145:13-16

WITH today's technology your work can follow you wherever you go. If you and your spouse don't set aside time for enjoying each other, you can easily spend every minute of every weekend on work that you brought home from the office and work around the house. The stress of constantly being "on call" can erode the foundation of love in our marriages. Although King David never knew the stresses of today's around-the-clock workplace, he did know what it meant to be burdened by too many responsibilities, to be bent low beneath a load. The image is of a person who's carrying too much. It could be a physical load—sacks of grain or a jar of water. But it could also refer to a heavy emotional load. Worries can weigh on people's minds to such an extent that those people act as if they're carrying a burden.

What burdens are you or your spouse carrying? Give those burdens to God. He is faithful and gracious and is able to lift your burdens when you give them to him.

PRAYING GOD'S PROMISE

Dear Lord, thank you for your faithfulness to us. You help the fallen. You lift up those burdened with loads. When my spouse falls, please come to the rescue. When my spouse is burdened, you lift up him or her and help to carry the load. You are gracious. You satisfy the hunger and thirst of everyone. Be gracious to us. We look to you for help. Open your hand and satisfy all our needs.

GOD'S PROMISE TO YOU

- God is faithful and gracious.
- He lifts up those who are bent beneath their loads.
- He helps those who have fallen.

THE PROMISE
GOD MEETS OUR NEEDS

Don't worry about everyday life—whether you have enough food, drink, and clothes. Doesn't life consist of more than food and clothing? . . . Can all your worries add a single moment to your life? Of course not. . . . Your heavenly Father already knows all your needs, and he will give you all you need from day to day if you live for him and make the Kingdom of God your primary concern.   Matthew 6:25-27, 32-33

O U R worries are often based on uncertainties. We don't know what surprises the future will bring, so we worry: Will we have enough money for the mortgage payment this month? Will our home or car need expensive repairs this year? Will my spouse or our children be injured in an accident? There are an infinite number of things we could spend our days worrying about. But Jesus tells us not to waste a moment worrying about the future. Worry doesn't solve a problem; in fact, worry sometimes makes a problem seem bigger than it is.

Jesus teaches us that instead of focusing on the problem, we are to commit our worries to God, who is all-powerful. He knows our needs. He wants to take care of those people who commit themselves to living for him day to day. Every morning commit your day to God and trust him for all that you need. Commit your spouse and his or her problems and worries to

God. Trust him to watch over and take care of your spouse. Your worrying won't help your spouse, but your prayers will.

PRAYING GOD'S PROMISE

Dear Lord, you promise that you will take care of our needs if we live for you each day. We want to live for you. We want to make your heavenly kingdom our primary concern. Take care of our needs, especially my spouse's needs, as you have promised. You tell us that we are valuable in your sight. You hold our futures. You know what will come tomorrow. I have no need to worry because you will look after my spouse's needs. I know that you have a plan, and I trust you to take care of us in the future. Help us to trust you even more.

GOD'S PROMISE TO YOU

- God considers you valuable in his sight.
- God already knows your needs.
- If you live for God, he will take care of all of your needs.

THE PROMISE
GOD RESCUES US FROM HARM

The eyes of the Lord watch over those who do right; his ears are open to their cries for help. . . . The Lord hears his people when they call to him for help. He rescues them from all their troubles. The Lord is close to the brokenhearted; he rescues those who are crushed in spirit. The righteous face many troubles, but the Lord rescues them from each and every one.

Psalm 34:15-19

G o d's Word describes life accurately. It's full of troubles. There are many dangers. Marriages experience rocky times. Some days you may have difficulty paying bills. On other days you and your spouse will be exhausted by all the things you have to do. You will almost certainly experience times of sorrow. The good news is that you can also look forward to times of rescue, refreshment, and rejoicing.

God's Word promises that God will give you and your spouse the strength to endure tough times (1 Peter 5:10). He promises to rescue those who are committed to following him. When your spirit is crushed, when you are brokenhearted over evil, look to God to rescue you from all of your troubles. Yes, you and your spouse will face many troubles in this life, but take heart; God is with you both. You and your spouse can remind each other that God is close by, that he's watching over you and planning your rescue.

PRAYING GOD'S PROMISE

Dear Lord, your Word promises that you are close to the brokenhearted. Your eyes are watching us; your ears hear us when we cry out for help. We're living for you, oh God. Watch over my spouse today. Hear my spouse's prayer and come to his or her rescue, as you have promised. Thank you for your nearness when we are brokenhearted. We rest in your presence with us. Please help my spouse to sense your nearness today.

GOD'S PROMISE TO YOU

- God watches over you and hears your cries for help.
- He is close to the brokenhearted.
- He will rescue you and protect you when you call to him.

THE PROMISE
GOD WILL NEVER FAIL US

Stay away from the love of money; be satisfied with what you have. For God has said, "I will never fail you. I will never forsake you." That is why we can say with confidence, "The Lord is my helper, so I will not be afraid. What can mere mortals do to me?" Remember your leaders who first taught you the word of God. Think of all the good that has come from their lives, and trust the Lord as they do. Jesus Christ is the same yesterday, today, and forever.   Hebrews 13:5-8

HAVE you ever felt abandoned? Maybe your friends weren't around in your time of need. Perhaps your family failed you when you needed them the most. Maybe the person you were sure you could always trust betrayed you. Those kinds of experiences leave us feeling frightened and insecure. If people experience feelings of abandonment too often, they may decide to give up on relationships with others and try to find a sense of security somewhere else—in "toys" or new cars or extravagant houses or professional success.

But contrary to what the world thinks, things do not give us security. According to the author of Hebrews, we won't find security in money; we can find security only in God, who will never fail us. The money we store up for ourselves can quickly disappear. Situations change—people have jobs one day and are unemployed the next. The stock market bottoms out, and money is gone as quickly as it came. We should certainly be responsible with our money, but we shouldn't depend on it for our security. God is our ultimate security because he never changes. He loves to provide for the needs of his people.

Your marriage will experience times of prosperity and times when money is scarce. Our job is to be content with what God has given us at each of those times and trust him to supply our needs. Make a commitment with each other that no matter what happens, you will rely on God for everything you need. Ask God to cultivate contentment in your hearts, and resolve to find your security in him.

PRAYING GOD'S PROMISE

Dear Lord, you promise you will never forsake us or fail us. We rest in that promise. Stay close to my spouse today, as your Word promises. Help us to trust in you, not in friends, family, or money. Help us to be content with what you've given us and to find true security as we rely on you for all that we need. Everything else may change, but you are the same yesterday, today, and forever.

GOD'S PROMISE TO YOU

- God will never fail you or forsake you.
- When he is your helper, you need not be afraid.
- He never changes.

THE PROMISE
GOD GIVES HIS PEOPLE SPECIAL GIFTS

Each of us has different work to do. . . . and each of us needs all the others. God has given each of us the ability to do certain things well. So if God has given you the ability to prophesy, speak out when you have faith that God is speaking through you. If your gift is that of serving others, serve them well. If you are a teacher, do a good job of teaching. If your gift is to encourage others, do it! If you have money, share it generously. If God has given you leadership ability, take the responsibility seriously. And if you have a gift for showing kindness to others, do it gladly. . . . Love each other with genuine affection, and take delight in honoring each other.   Romans 12:5-10

D o you know someone who is difficult to get along with? Maybe he's talkative in the morning when you really need silence. Maybe she's someone who second-guesses your decisions. Maybe he's impetuous, quick to act without considering the consequences of his actions. When you're married, it's easy to find some habit in your spouse that grates on your nerves. But often the same traits that cause irritation also make a person very good at a special task. The person who talks in the morning may be a great speaker. The person who second-guesses you may be a brilliant analyst. The impetuous person may be an artist who is able to take risks for the sake of creativity.

The apostle Paul understood that differences between people could cause division in the church. That is why he reminded the Romans that people's differences can complement and help each other. This is true in marriage as well. God has made two unique individuals into one. Each spouse has special gifts from God. Spouses need to celebrate those differences and gifts and honor each other for who God has created them to be.

Thank God for the special abilities and gifts your spouse has, and decide to celebrate the ways you and your spouse complement each other because you are different.

PRAYING GOD'S PROMISE

Dear Lord, you have made us to belong to each other and need each other. Thank you for giving each one of us abilities to do certain things well. Thank you for creating us for each other. Help us to recognize and honor the differences you have created in each one of us. Your Word promises that you have a good plan for us. We are glad for that good plan, and we ask you to help us to submit to it. Guide us today as you have promised.

GOD'S PROMISE TO YOU

- God has made us to meet the needs of others.
- Each of us has special abilities from God.
- He wants us to use our gifts and abilities.

THE PROMISE
GOD UPHOLDS US

I have called you back from the ends of the earth so you can serve me. For I have chosen you and will not throw you away. Don't be afraid, for I am with you. Do not be dismayed, for I am your God. I will strengthen you. I will help you. I will uphold you with my victorious right hand. . . . I am holding you by your right hand—I, the Lord your God.

Isaiah 41:9-10, 13

"I am holding you by your right hand." God made this promise to the Israelites through the prophet Isaiah. Even though God warned them that they would be scattered throughout the world because of their sins, Isaiah spoke of a day when God would call them back to serve God once again. God promised to be with those people he had called and to help them. As believers, we can claim these promises because God has called us to be his holy people and to serve him (1 Peter 2:9). God has given us the same promises. He will never abandon us (Psalm 27:10). He will be with us; he will strengthen us and come to our rescue (Psalm 59:9). Our Lord doesn't simply help us. He sustains and upholds us. He stands next to us, holding our right hand. He is ready to help us when we call on him (Psalm 55:16).

Do you or your spouse feel weak? Is there a situation that worries you? Remind yourselves of God's promises. God stands next to your spouse to help and to give strength. And he upholds both of you each and every day.

PRAYING GOD'S PROMISE

Dear Lord, you promise to be with those of us you have called to serve you. You promise to strengthen us. Thank you for calling us to be your people, just as you called the Israelites. We want to serve you. Be close to us, as you have promised. Strengthen me and my spouse for service. We ask you to be near us and help us. Uphold both my spouse and me with your victorious right hand, and help us to know and do your will today.

GOD'S PROMISE TO YOU

- God is with the people he has called.
- He will strengthen you to serve him.
- God will uphold you with his mighty hand.

THE PROMISE
GOD SHEPHERDS US

The Lord is my shepherd; I have everything I need. He lets me rest in green meadows; he leads me beside peaceful streams. He renews my strength. He guides me along right paths, bringing honor to his name. . . . You welcome me as a guest, anointing my head with oil. My cup overflows with blessings. Surely your goodness and unfailing love will pursue me all the days of my life. Psalm 23:1-6

G O D created us with the need for rest and relaxation. Too often, though, we try to ignore the cries of our bodies and spirits for times of rest. We push ourselves to meet impossible deadlines. We cram too much into our days. But it wasn't God's design for us to live frantic lives. In his law he set aside a full day every week for rest (Exodus 20:8-11). He knew that we need time to rejuvenate our bodies and our souls. We need time to refocus our lives on God and on what's eternal. When David described God as his shepherd in Psalm 23, he portrays God as guiding him to times of rest. It was during those times that God renewed David's strength so that he could continue the journey God had before him. Those times of rest didn't keep David from a full life. No, just the opposite! David describes his life as overflowing with God's blessing.

Are you careful to set aside time to rest every week? You and your spouse need to agree to take time to enjoy each other and to enjoy God. This can be difficult to do with crowded schedules, but it's necessary if you're to be able to recharge and renew yourselves for the challenges you'll face. Ask God today to help you and your spouse schedule times of rest and refreshment into your week.

PRAYING GOD'S PROMISE

Dear Lord, your Word promises that you supply all of our needs, including our need for rest. You promise that you will renew our strength. You know our needs. Grant us what we need so we can continue to serve you. Help my spouse and me to find time to rest. Refresh us and give us rest. Your Word promises that you will fill our lives with blessings, that you will love us and provide us with good things. I know you are good and that you want to fill our lives with your blessings. Help my spouse and me to recognize your blessings and praise you for them.

GOD'S PROMISE TO YOU

- God is your shepherd.
- He will guide you along right paths.
- He will give you rest and renew your strength.

THE PROMISE
GOD FULFILLS THE DESIRES OF HIS PEOPLE

The Lord is close to all who call on him, yes, to all who call on him sincerely. He fulfills the desires of those who fear him; he hears their cries for help and rescues them. The Lord protects all those who love him, but he destroys the wicked. I will praise the Lord, and everyone on earth will bless his holy name forever and forever. Psalm 145:18-21

W HEN we speak of our desires, often we mean those desires that pull us down and lead us astray. Those desires can have both a good and a bad side. On the negative side, our desire for significance can lead us to selfishly grab for power in the corporate world. But when we commit ourselves to God, he can use that same impulse in expanding his kingdom in this world. Our desire for security may motivate us to hoard wealth. But when we submit that desire to God, he can use it to motivate us to ask him every day for what we need and to look to him for protection.

A wicked desire is a perversion of what God made to be good. He created us with desires, and he is the only one we can expect to fulfill our deepest yearnings. We may not know exactly how God will fulfill our desires, but because we know that he has a good plan for us, we can trust him to do it in the way that is best for us.

What do you and your spouse deeply yearn for? It's good to discuss these desires—both good and bad—with your spouse. Then, together, you can give those desires to God and wait for God to provide.

PRAYING GOD'S PROMISE

Dear Lord, your Word promises that you are close to everyone who calls on you. We call on you today. I pray that you will watch over my spouse and be close to him or her. You promise to fulfill the desires of those who fear you and to protect those who love you. We love you, Lord, and we respect your name. We want to follow your ways. Please fulfill the pure desires you have placed in my spouse's heart.

GOD'S PROMISE TO YOU

- God is close to those who call on him.
- He will fulfill the desires of those who fear him.
- He protects those who love him.

THE PROMISE
GOD WORKS EVERYTHING OUT FOR OUR GOOD

The Holy Spirit helps us in our distress. For we don't even know what we should pray for, nor how we should pray. But the Holy Spirit prays for us with groanings that cannot be expressed in words. And the Father who knows all hearts knows what the Spirit is saying, for the Spirit pleads for us believers in harmony with God's own will. And we know that God causes everything to work together for the good of those who love God and are called according to his purpose for them.

Romans 8:26-28

WE'VE all seen people who are so exhausted or so wounded that they can't help themselves. An exhausted runner who desperately needs water can't drink it without assistance. A person in shock after a car accident wanders around in a daze instead of seeking medical assistance. The same type of thing happens in our spiritual life. In times of distress we can be so emotionally exhausted that we don't know what to pray for.

As believers we have the Holy Spirit within us, who helps us when we're distressed. The Spirit seeks help for us when we can't do it for ourselves. This can be a great source of comfort. God doesn't abandon us when we don't know what to pray for or don't have the strength to voice the cries of our hearts. That certainly doesn't mean we should abandon trying to pray. Yet it does mean that we don't have to censor our prayers. We can freely admit our weaknesses, our sins, our desires to God, for God knows our hearts. We can be assured that he is working out his good plan for us because in the midst of our distress the Holy Spirit is praying for us "in harmony with God's will."

If you or your spouse is experiencing a time of distress, take time now to lay every one of your problems in front of God. Ask him to calm your fears and to help you to trust that he is working everything out for your good, even if you can't see it right now.

PRAYING GOD'S PROMISE

Dear Lord, your Word promises that the Holy Spirit helps us when we're distressed. We love you. Thank you for placing your Holy Spirit within us. When my spouse and I are distressed, work out your good purpose for us. You know our hearts. They are open to you, oh God. We want to follow your will. Thank you for the assurance that when we can't seem to pray for ourselves, your Holy Spirit is praying for us. Please make the difficult situations we're experiencing work out for our ultimate good.

GOD'S PROMISE TO YOU

- The Holy Spirit will help you in times of distress.
- God knows what is in your hearts.
- God will work everything out for your good.

THE PROMISE
GOD WILL TAKE CARE OF US

Fear and trembling overwhelm me. I can't stop shaking. Oh,
how I wish I had wings like a dove; then I would fly away
and rest! I would fly far away to the quiet of the wilderness.
. . . But I will call on God, and the Lord will rescue me.
Morning, noon, and night I plead aloud in my distress, and the
Lord hears my voice. . . . Give your burdens to the Lord, and
he will take care of you. He will not permit the godly to slip
and fall.   Psalm 55:5-7, 16-17, 22

H A V E you ever wished that you could just sprout wings and fly
far away from a difficult situation? Maybe your workload is too
great and you feel as if you can't handle it. Maybe you said the
wrong thing to an important person. Maybe you feel
surrounded by people who want to see you fail. David, the
author of Psalm 55, felt that way. In today's verses he isn't
afraid to tell God that he wants to "fly far away." Yet David
knew that flying away wasn't the solution. Praying to God and
asking him for rescue was the only way David would find relief.
Morning, noon, and night, he pleaded for help. And God heard.
He lifted David's burden. He protected David from falling. God
promises to do the same for every one who lives for him.

If you follow him, God is listening to your prayers. He is willing and more than able to rescue you, to lift your burdens, and to take care of you and your spouse.

One of the best ways you can communicate love to your spouse is by praying for him or her. What burdens are you or your spouse carrying right now? Take time to pray about them, especially your spouse's burdens.

PRAYING GOD'S PROMISE

Dear Lord, your Word promises that you hear those who ask you for help and that you rescue them. As your children, we call on you for help. Hear us, as you have promised you will. Rescue my spouse and me from the trouble that surrounds us. You promise to take care of the burdens of the godly. You promise to protect us from falling. Oh Lord, I give you my burdens and the burdens of my spouse today. Remind my spouse of your promise of care and protection.

GOD'S PROMISE TO YOU

- God will hear and rescue those who call on him.
- He will take care of your burdens.
- He won't allow you to slip and fall.

THE PROMISE
GOD GRANTS SUCCESS

Teach us to make the most of our time, so that we may grow in wisdom. . . . And may the Lord our God show us his approval and make our efforts successful.　　　Psalm 90:12, 17

ALTHOUGH we can't see or feel time, it rules our lives. Every moment we spend doing one thing—whether it's working or resting, reading books or playing tennis—is a moment we can't spend on some other worthwhile endeavor. While we're on this earth, we're limited by the number of years God has granted us (Psalm 90:10). That is why Moses, the author of Psalm 90, asks God to teach him to make the most of his time.

The Bible tells us that God grants wisdom to those who ask him for it (James 1:5), and Moses knew that wonderful truth. Moses knew that if he and the Israelites sought God's will, committed their plans to God, and followed God's ways, God would shower his favor on them. He would lead them to use their time doing things that were worthwhile, things that would last for all eternity. Their work would be successful because God was in it.

We can claim these promises for us today if we wholeheartedly follow God. Take time to commit the plans you and your spouse have to God. Ask him to direct you and to be in your work. Don't be afraid to ask for success. God wants to bless people who love and obey him.

PRAYING GOD'S PROMISE

Dear Lord, your Word promises that you will give your wisdom to those who ask for it. Give my spouse and me wisdom in how we use our time. May we spend our time and energies on what will last. You have said that you will grant success to those who commit their plans and ways to you. We commit our plans for our life together to you, oh God. Please make our efforts successful.

GOD'S PROMISE TO YOU

- God will give you wisdom if you ask him for it.
- When you commit your way to God, he will grant success to your efforts.

THE PROMISE
GOD GIVES TO THOSE WHO GIVE

Honor the Lord with your wealth and with the best part of everything your land produces. Then he will fill your barns with grain, and your vats will overflow with the finest wine.

Proverbs 3:9-10

Bills, bills, bills. If your household is like most, every day seems to bring another bill in the mail. Everything from the mortgage to the phone bill eats away at your checking account, not leaving much money for the daily coffee-and-muffin break.

The Bible teaches that your first priority when it comes to managing your money should be giving a portion—in fact, the best part—to God. Why is this so important? Because everything you have, from your job to your car to the clothes in your closet to your coffee and muffin, is a gift from God. He is the One who not only enables the crops to grow but also gives you the ability to work effectively. One way you can acknowledge your complete dependence on him is to give a portion back, as a sacrifice of thanksgiving. By giving the best part to God, you're demonstrating your wholehearted gratitude for all he has given you.

The Bible teaches that God rewards those who make it a first priority to give back to him. Set aside time this week to pray about your budget. Thank God for all of his financial blessings on your marriage, and ask him what portion you and your spouse should commit to giving to the church and even to other ministries. As you give, remind yourselves of this promise that God will reward your sacrifice.

PRAYING GOD'S PROMISE

Dear Lord, your Word promises that you bless those who honor you with their wealth. We know that everything we have is a gift from you. We commit to giving the best of everything we have back to you. Help us to be faithful in honoring that commitment because you are always faithful to provide for us. May we know your blessing on our sacrifice.

GOD'S PROMISE TO YOU

● God blesses those who honor him with their wealth.

THE PROMISE
GOD FILLS LIFE WITH GOODNESS

Praise the Lord, I tell myself; with my whole heart, I will praise his holy name. Praise the Lord, I tell myself, and never forget the good things he does for me. He forgives all my sins and heals all my diseases. He ransoms me from death and surrounds me with love and tender mercies. He fills my life with good things. My youth is renewed like the eagle's!

Psalm 103:1-5

HAVE you ever tried to count your blessings? In this psalm David describes his genuine contentment with what God has given him. He praises the Lord for what he has given him and for the "good things" God has done for him. And he praises God for the greatest gift—the forgiveness of his sin. Make a list of all the good things God has given you and your spouse. Thank him with all your heart for those good gifts in your life.

While it's not wrong for us to ask our heavenly Father to bless us in a particular way or to give us something we long for, God is pleased with those who are content with the good gifts he's already given. So before you ask for more, first think about and acknowledge the good things God has given you, just as David did. Praise God for salvation from sin, the gift of eternal life, his unfailing love, his faithful provision, your spouse, etc. Encourage yourself, as David did, to "never forget the good things he does" for you.

PRAYING GOD'S PROMISE

Dear Lord God, we read in your Word that you will forgive all our sins if we turn away from them and ask for forgiveness. You will ransom us from death if we believe in your Son. Thank you for sending Jesus to pay for our sins. We thank you for all of your good gifts to us—our marriage, our home, and especially the precious gift of salvation. Help us never to forget your good gifts. Please continue to bless my spouse and our marriage.

GOD'S PROMISE TO YOU

- God forgives those who turn away from their sins.
- He has paid the price to rescue his people from death.
- He delights in giving his people good things.

THE PROMISE
GOD HELPS US TO RESIST TEMPTATION

If you think you are standing strong, be careful, for you, too, may fall into . . . sin. But remember that the temptations that come into your life are no different from what others experience. And God is faithful. He will keep the temptation from becoming so strong that you can't stand up against it. When you are tempted, he will show you a way out so that you will not give in to it.   1 Corinthians 10:12-13

SOMETIMES temptation seems impossible to resist. Television, magazines, and radio programs can all become sources of temptation. Whether we're struggling with anger or sexual sin, the devil can use the things we come across every day to tempt us. When we're tempted, we feel very weak and incapable of standing up against the temptation. Left to ourselves, that's true. But we must remember that God is the strong one. He's on our side, and he wants to show us how to resist temptation.

As we consistently depend on God to help us resist temptation, we may start to feel as if we have "conquered" that sin when in reality, it is God who has been supplying the strength to help us resist that temptation day after day. That's why the apostle Paul encourages us never to think that we're standing strong on our own. We should never become confident in our own ability to live pure and holy lives. The Bible states that as soon as we grow proud in our abilities, we will fall (Proverbs 18:12). God will not support and uphold us when we grow proud because we're not depending on him alone; instead, we're trying to live life in our own power, and that's a recipe for disaster.

Pray today that God will strengthen you and your spouse to bear up against temptation. Ask him to show you and your spouse the way to escape temptation.

PRAYING GOD'S PROMISE

Dear God, your Word promises that you won't allow temptation to grow too strong for us. You will always remain faithful to us and help us to guard our hearts. May we never grow proud because we think that we're standing strong on our own. Strengthen us and protect us from the temptations we face every day. Thank you for providing a way out when we face them. Please strengthen my spouse and me so that we can recognize temptation when it comes and look to you for a way to escape it. Help us to live by your power, not our own.

GOD'S PROMISE TO YOU

- God is faithful to his people.
- He will keep temptation from becoming too strong for you.
- He will show you how you can escape temptation.

THE PROMISE
GOD PROTECTS THOSE WHO TRUST IN HIM

If you make the Lord your refuge, if you make the Most High your shelter, no evil will conquer you; no plague will come near your dwelling. For he orders his angels to protect you wherever you go. They will hold you with their hands to keep you from striking your foot on a stone. . . . The Lord says, "I will rescue those who love me. I will protect those who trust in my name. When they call on me, I will answer; I will be with them in trouble. I will rescue them and honor them. I will satisfy them with a long life and give them my salvation."

Psalm 91:9-12, 14-16

WANDER into any card store these days, and you'll see chubby little angels smiling up at you from a card. Today's verses speak of angels. But their description of angels differs from the popular depiction of round little toddlers with wings. The Bible typically describes angels as warriors and messengers, sometimes depicting them with swords drawn (Numbers 22:23). Angels obey the commands of the mighty King of kings. They protect God's followers from danger (Psalm 91:11), and they deliver important messages from God (Judges 13).

Ancient Israel was a dangerous place. Wealthy people hired armed guards to protect them from thieves and robbers. Yet in today's passage the Lord promises that those who trust him wholeheartedly enjoy the protection and watchful care of God's mighty angelic warriors. That's an amazing promise! But what's even more amazing is that God himself promises to come to the rescue of those who love him and to protect those who trust in him. He promises to be with those who call on him in trouble. Much more amazing than angels standing beside us is the fact that God cares enough to save us.

Have you thought about what it means to have God's angels protect you and your spouse? Have you thought about how comforting God's protection can be? As you pray today, reaffirm your trust in God alone, and then rest in his promise of protection for you and your spouse.

PRAYING GOD'S PROMISE

Dear God, your Word promises that if we make you our refuge and shelter, you will order your angels to protect us wherever we go. We want to live under your protective care. Please send your angels to protect my spouse today. You promise to rescue those who love you, to protect those who trust you, and to answer those who call on you. We thank you for being with us in our troubles. We do love you. Answer us when we call on you, as you have promised to do. Keep my spouse from trouble, and grant your protection.

GOD'S PROMISE TO YOU

- God will rescue and protect you if you love him.
- He will answer you when you call on him and will give you his salvation.

THE PROMISE
GOD NEVER ABANDONS US

This precious treasure—this light and power that now shine within us—is held in perishable containers, that is, in our weak bodies. So everyone can see that our glorious power is from God and is not our own. We are pressed on every side by troubles, but we are not crushed and broken. We are perplexed, but we don't give up and quit. We are hunted down, but God never abandons us. We get knocked down, but we get up again and keep going. Through suffering, these bodies of ours constantly share in the death of Jesus so that the life of Jesus may also be seen in our bodies.   2 Corinthians 4:7-10

H A V E you ever felt like the apostle Paul? Troubles on every side. Crushed and broken. Even hunted down. You may never experience the severe persecution that Paul faced, but you have access to the same source of power Paul had. The same God who never abandoned Paul is the God you worship. Paul could hold up under the strain of persecution because God upheld him. Just as Paul had the light and power of God within his body, so you, too, as a believer have the Holy Spirit within you.

The Holy Spirit shines within you, illuminating God's truth and showing you God's ways (John 16:12-15). Although your body may be weak, you have an eternal source of power within your soul because of the Holy Spirit in you. And he will never abandon you. When you feel weak, he will strengthen you (1 Peter 5:10). When you feel confused, he will guide you and give you wisdom (James 1:5). When you have God's Spirit, you are never alone in your difficulties.

Ask God today for the inner strength you and your spouse need to endure suffering and difficulties. The Lord your God will help you, and others will see Christ in you as you submit to the Spirit's guidance.

PRAYING GOD'S PROMISE

Dear God, you have promised that you will place a precious treasure—your very glory—within us. Thank you for giving us your light and power to guide and strengthen us. Help us to reflect your gifts and your glory so that others will see Jesus in us. Your Word promises that you will never abandon us. We are pressed by troubles and demands. We are often perplexed. Thank you for never leaving us. Stay close to us, oh God. Strengthen us to endure the troubles we face.

GOD'S PROMISE TO YOU

- God puts his precious treasure—his light and power—in his people to show that our power comes from him and not from ourselves.
- He will never abandon you in times of trouble.

THE PROMISE
GOD WILL PROVIDE PEACE

Don't worry about anything; instead, pray about everything. Tell God what you need, and thank him for all he has done. If you do this, you will experience God's peace, which is far more wonderful than the human mind can understand. His peace will guard your hearts and minds as you live in Christ Jesus.

Philippians 4:6-7

THERE are times in our lives when it's extraordinarily difficult to calm our racing hearts. A crisis may have arisen at work. Maybe someone close to us is experiencing deep trouble. Or sometimes we just feel stuck trying to juggle the constant flow of demands on our time without ever getting the chance to take a break. During those times our hearts can be anything but peaceful. Anxiety grips our hearts and minds. Our thoughts can become wild and erratic. We may feel lost and abandoned.

The good news is, there is relief. The Bible promises that if instead of worrying about what is bothering us, we pray about it, the peace of God will wash over our hearts and minds. We may not experience peace right away, but when we consistently commit our concerns and anxiety to God in prayer, he will release us from their grip on our hearts. It's a promise. You'll learn how to trust God with your future, your spouse's future, and the future of your closest friends. You'll know without a doubt that God plans only the best for you (Psalm 32:8).

Are there areas in your marriage that you worry about? Are you concerned about your spouse? Instead of worrying, pray about those things, and ask God to give you his peace.

PRAYING GOD'S PROMISE

Dear Lord, your Word promises that we will experience your peace if we ask you for what we need. We don't understand your peace, but we need it. Thank you for meeting our needs in the past. We give you our worries and concerns. Grant my spouse and me peace of mind as we move ahead in your name. Your Word promises that as we live for Jesus, your peace will guard our hearts and minds. Help us to live for you, Jesus. Keep us from worry as we realize that you are in control and want only the best for us.

GOD'S PROMISE TO YOU

- When you pray, you will experience God's peace.
- God will guard your hearts and minds.

PART 3

PRAYING GOD'S PROMISES FOR OUR HOME

WHEN two lives are woven together by marriage, a unique space is created by their love. You can see this when you walk into a couple's home. It bears the imprint of both the husband's and the wife's personalities. The state-of-the-art stereo system in the corner of the family room may reflect the husband's passion for music while the living room's decor reflects the wife's interests in flowers or art. If each of these people were living alone, the space might look very different. But together a husband and wife create a unique place where they communicate and demonstrate their love for each other and their devotion to sharing their lives. Every marriage has a special purpose, and God has a unique plan for every couple. The loving atmosphere in a home has a huge impact on any children the couple may have, and warm hospitality and compassion can influence a neighborhood with God's love (Psalm 112:1-2).

You may not realize the impact your home—whether it's a one-bedroom apartment in the city, a condo, or a sprawling ranch house in the suburbs—has on those who enter it. But God wants to use it. Pray about the type of home environment you are creating. Everything you do and say affects the atmosphere in your home. Will it be a loving and caring place? Or will it be a place of division, discord, and complaining? Spend this month praying God's promises for your home, and ask him to make it a place that reflects his love.

THE PROMISE
GOD'S SPIRIT PRODUCES KINDNESS

When the Holy Spirit controls our lives, he will produce this
kind of fruit in us: love, joy, peace, patience, kindness, goodness,
faithfulness, gentleness, and self-control. Here there is no conflict
with the law. Those who belong to Christ Jesus have nailed the
passions and desires of their sinful nature to his cross and
crucified them there. If we are living now by the Holy Spirit,
let us follow the Holy Spirit's leading in every part of our lives.
Let us not become conceited, or irritate one another, or be jealous of one another.   Galatians 5:22-26

How do you remember your childhood home? Was it a loving
and welcoming place? Maybe there were evidences of kindness
and generosity—fresh homemade cookies, a dollhouse or model
planes you and your dad built together, a warm welcome always
waiting for you, an old couch to be shared with brothers and
sisters.

Perhaps you don't have such wonderful childhood memories.
Not everyone does. Homes can be places of cruelty as
well—places full of criticism and humiliation, places characterized by conflict, jealousy, and pain. Loving homes don't just
magically appear. They are the result of a husband and wife's
commitment to letting God's Spirit control their lives. When
you follow the Spirit's leading, God produces kindness, good-

ness, patience, and love in your lives. Then the home your marriage creates can become a light to your neighborhood, a place where your friends and neighbors can experience genuine love and acceptance. What type of home do you want your marriage to create? Ask God today to plant the seeds of loving-kindness in your life, your marriage, and your home.

PRAYING GOD'S PROMISE

Dear Lord, your Word promises that your Spirit will produce kindness, goodness, and self-control in our lives. We need that and want that in our home. Please fill it with patience, kindness, and goodness. Your Word promises that those who belong to you can nail their sinful passions and desires to your cross. Help us to crucify our sinful habits and selfish desires and to follow the Spirit's leading in our lives. Help us to create a home where your Spirit rules.

GOD'S PROMISE TO YOU

- God's Spirit will produce kindness and goodness in your life.
- He will help you to crucify your sinful desires.

THE PROMISE
HAPPINESS IS FOUND IN GOD'S LAW

Make me walk along the path of your commands, for that is where my happiness is found. Give me an eagerness for your decrees; do not inflict me with love for money! Turn my eyes from worthless things, and give me life through your word. Reassure me of your promise, which is for those who honor you. Psalm 119:35-38

W HERE do we find genuine happiness? In wealth? In success? In fame? Television and magazines try to convince us that money, fame, and success are the source of happiness. But we all know of a rich person whose personal life is a shambles, a successful businessman who has had a midlife crisis and left his wife and children, a famous music star who has traded fame for the hypnotic effect of drugs and alcohol.

According to the Bible, genuine happiness is the result of following God faithfully all the days of our lives. It's difficult to find a godly person who regrets doing that. The lure of glamour, fame, and wealth can dazzle us into forgetting what will bring us true happiness: following God day in and day out. That's why the psalmist asked God to keep him from the "love of money" and his eyes from "worthless things." Just as the psalmist did, we need to ask God for "eagerness" for what's true, right, and eternal because sometimes we're drawn to the glitz of "worthless things." Ask God to make your home a place that prizes him and his truth.

PRAYING GOD'S PROMISE

Dear Lord God, your Word promises that happiness is found in walking along the path of your commands. Help us to do that instead of being driven by a love for money. Grant us happiness and joy in our home, as your Word promises. You promise life through your Word. Your promises are for those who honor you. We want to honor you alone, oh God, by following your Word. Grant us abundant life as we live for you.

GOD'S PROMISE TO YOU

- Those who walk according to God's law will find happiness.
- God grants life through his Word.
- Those who honor him will experience the fulfillment of his promises.

THE PROMISE
GOD'S LOVE REMAINS WITH US

Can anything ever separate us from Christ's love? Does it mean he no longer loves us if we have trouble or calamity, or are persecuted, or are hungry or cold or in danger or threatened with death? . . . I am convinced that nothing can ever separate us from his love. . . . Our fears for today, our worries about tomorrow, and even the powers of hell can't keep God's love away. Romans 8:35, 38

HAVE you ever felt that someone's love for you was conditional? It's sad but true that many of us are used to feeling that way. We just naturally think someone's affection depends on how we look or how we act or what we can do for that person. We live with the fear that if we do something wrong—or don't do something we should—we may lose that friendship or affection.

Today's verses show us an entirely different type of love. Jesus loved us when we were his enemies (Romans 5:6-8). He continues to love us despite the fact that we can never do anything to be worthy of that love. No matter what happens, whether it's financial trouble or natural disasters, you can be assured that as a believer you have God's love seeing you through. There's no reason to worry or fear. Jesus is near and is looking out for you. Nothing can make him stop loving you.

That's the same type of love you and your spouse should have for each other. It's called unconditional love. Unconditional love sees potential underneath obvious flaws or weaknesses. Unconditional love makes sacrifices without ever expecting anything in return. Unconditional love should be the bedrock of every marriage and home. Ask God to teach you and your spouse how to demonstrate unconditional love to each other and to anyone else who enters your home.

PRAYING GOD'S PROMISE

Dear Jesus, your Word promises that nothing—not even death or life—can separate us from your love when we belong to you. Thank you for loving us unconditionally. We commit to you everything that distracts us from concentrating on your love for us—our worries and fears, dangers and threats, troubles and calamities. We believe your love will never leave us. Help us to have that type of love for each other. Despite the troubles we may experience in this life, victory is ours through you. No matter how bad things may seem, keep us focused on your great love for us.

GOD'S PROMISE TO YOU

- Nothing can ever separate you from God's love.

THE PROMISE
GOD GIVES JOY

[Jesus said,] "I am the vine; you are the branches. Those who remain in me, and I in them, will produce much fruit. . . . If you stay joined to me and my words remain in you, you may ask any request you like, and it will be granted! My true disciples produce much fruit. This brings great glory to my Father. . . . When you obey me, you remain in my love, just as I obey my Father and remain in his love. I have told you this so that you will be filled with my joy. Yes, your joy will overflow!

John 15:5-11

A healthy tree is pruned on a regular basis. The gardener identifies the branches that are sapping strength from the tree and cuts them off. The tree itself grows stronger because of the pruning, but anything the gardener cuts off quickly turns brown and dies. Branches and buds separated from the roots that provide nourishment can't live for long. They're good only for the waste pile.

Jesus compares believers to branches. Connected to Jesus, the vine, we can grow green and produce much fruit. Apart from Jesus, we're nothing. That's why so many promises in Scripture are connected to whether we're following Jesus. With Jesus, we receive God's blessing. Our work has significance (Psalm 90:17), our families are secure (Psalm 32:7), and we experience God's joy. Our homes become places where we rejoice in God's gifts instead of places where criticism and complaining abound. We can see our spouses as God's gifts to us, and our joy overflows from our home into the lives of the people we touch.

If your spouse is not a believer, don't lose heart. God's Word promises that your relationship with God will sanctify your home (1 Corinthians 7:14). Your own joy that comes from staying close to Christ will make its mark in your home.

PRAYING GOD'S PROMISE

Dear Jesus, you promise to make us fruitful. You promise that our prayers will be granted if we remain in you. Make our marriage and home fruitful. Keep us always close to you so that we can produce lasting fruit. You promise overflowing joy for those who remain in your love. Protect us from wandering from your love. Give us hearts that desire to obey you. Make our home one that is filled to overflowing with the joy that comes from you.

GOD'S PROMISE TO YOU

- When you remain in God, you will bear fruit and bring God great glory.
- When you remain in God's love, you will experience overflowing joy.

THE PROMISE
GOD IS OUR REFUGE

Those who live in the shelter of the Most High will find rest in the shadow of the Almighty. This I declare of the Lord: He alone is my refuge, my place of safety; he is my God, and I am trusting him. For he will rescue you from every trap and protect you from the fatal plague. He will shield you with his wings. He will shelter you with his feathers. His faithful promises are your armor and protection. Do not be afraid of the terrors of the night, nor fear the dangers of the day.

Psalm 91:1-5

T HIS world isn't scary only for kids. It can be scary for adults as well. The evening news broadcasts the worst in our communities—carjackings, burglaries, murders. The Bible acknowledges the "dangers of the day" and "the terrors of the night" that can frighten anyone. But it also encourages us to look to God for protection from those things. We are to depend on him alone for our safety. We tend to think of our homes as places of shelter and safety, but we need to acknowledge that God is the One who *truly* shelters us. His promises are like armor because he always backs them up with action. He never goes back on his word. He is always with us. That's why it's so important for us to know God's promises and to pray those promises for our home. Ask God to help you and your spouse to find your confidence and shelter in him.

PRAYING GOD'S PROMISE

Dear Lord, you promise to rescue and protect us. You are our God. We trust you to protect our home as you have promised. Oh God, you promise to be our refuge, our shelter, and our place of safety. You alone are our refuge. May you shield us with your wings, and shelter us with your feathers. May you make our home a place of safety.

GOD'S PROMISE TO YOU

- God is able to rescue you and protect you.
- He will be your refuge, your shield, and your true place of safety.

THE PROMISE
GOD DELIGHTS IN THOSE
WHO KEEP THEIR WORD

Some people make cutting remarks, but the words of the wise bring healing. Truth stands the test of time; lies are soon exposed. Deceit fills hearts that are plotting evil; joy fills hearts that are planning peace! No real harm befalls the godly, but the wicked have their fill of trouble. The Lord hates those who don't keep their word, but he delights in those who do.

Proverbs 12:18-22

T H E quickest way to destroy a marriage and the loving atmosphere of a home is with cutting and untruthful words. When we allow ourselves to cut down our spouses with a flippant response or unloving words, we're attacking the very foundation of our marriages. It's even worse when we intentionally deceive one another. Love and trust in marriage are built on complete openness and honesty with one another. That means we have to be entirely truthful with each other and refrain from remarks or responses that demean the other person or show disrespect.

A quick retort may inspire laughter in a sitcom, but we can't build trust in a marriage when we're putting our spouses or other family members down. James describes the tongue as "an uncontrollable evil, full of deadly poison. Sometimes it praises our Lord and Father, and sometimes it breaks out into curses against those who have been made in the image of God" (James 3:8-9). We need to be extremely careful about what comes out of our lips. God hears and judges every word we speak (Matthew 12:36-37).

The Bible tells us that God delights in those whose words are pure and that wise people use healing, helpful, and gentle words to cover wrongs and wounds (Proverbs 15:26). Pray that your home will be filled with encouraging and healing words so that God may delight in it.

PRAYING GOD'S PROMISE

Dear Lord, your Word promises that no real harm will fall on the godly and that the truth will stand the test of time. We want to live for you, telling the truth and speaking healing words. Please protect us from harm. Your Word promises that you delight in those who tell the truth and keep their word. Help us to be truthful with each other and to encourage honesty in our home so that you can take delight in it.

GOD'S PROMISE TO YOU

- God delights in those who keep their word.

THE PROMISE
GOD HEARS THE PRAYERS OF THE HUMBLE

If my people who are called by my name will humble themselves and pray and seek my face and turn from their wicked
ways, I will hear from heaven and will forgive their sins and
heal their land. I will listen to every prayer made in this place.

2 Chronicles 7:14-15

God gave this promise to King Solomon after the dedication of
the temple. Solomon prayed that God's ears would always be
"attentive to all the prayers made to you [God] in this place"
(2 Chronicles 6:40). It's okay to ask God to listen to our prayers.
King Solomon and King David did it (Psalm 28:2).

Even though God has given us many promises in Scripture
that he will hear those who call on him (Psalm 116:2), it is good
to remind ourselves what a miracle it is that God, who created
and rules the cosmos, listens to us. When Solomon asked God
to listen to the people's prayers, God answered Solomon with a
resounding yes, as long as his people were humble and repentant and relied on God for mercy.

Our own requests for God to listen to us receive the same
gracious yes. We can know with absolute certainty that God is
listening (Isaiah 65:24). Just as Solomon prayed that the temple
would become a house of prayer, you can ask God to make your
home a house of prayer. You can ask God to make you and your

spouse people of prayer—people who take seriously the privilege of entering God's presence and communicating with him.

PRAYING GOD'S PROMISE

Dear Lord, you promise to hear from heaven those who seek you with humble, repentant hearts. We are humbly seeking you. We want your will for us. Hear and answer our prayers. Make our home a house of prayer. You promise to forgive and heal those who turn from their wicked ways. We confess our sin to you. Please forgive us, and heal our marriage and our home.

GOD'S PROMISE TO YOU

- God listens to those who humbly seek him.
- He forgives those who turn from their sins.

THE PROMISE
GOD GIVES GOOD GIFTS

[Jesus said,] "Keep on asking, and you will be given what you ask for. Keep on looking, and you will find. Keep on knocking, and the door will be opened. For everyone who asks, receives. Everyone who seeks, finds. And the door is opened to everyone who knocks. . . . If you sinful people know how to give good gifts to your children, how much more will your heavenly Father give good gifts to those who ask him."

Matthew 7:7-8, 11

GOD's wisdom is very different from ours. What would this passage sound like if a contemporary businessman or professor rewrote it? Perhaps, "Keep on working, and you'll receive what you want." Maybe, "Go ahead and turn the handle, and the door will open." In sharp contrast, Jesus tells us to keep on seeking God, knocking at his door, and asking him for what we need. In God's eyes it's not what we do but whom we depend on that matters.

We can work as hard as we want, but if God doesn't bless our work, our efforts will be futile (Psalm 90:17). We can try to figure out where we want to go, but if God doesn't direct our steps, we will just be wandering around in circles. We can try to open doors for ourselves, but if God hasn't opened the door first, we may find it slammed in our faces.

On the other hand, if we go to God *first* and continue to go to him, he will open doors for us. If we keep on asking him for what we need, he will provide good gifts for us. If we truly seek him, we will find him.

PRAYING GOD'S PROMISE

Dear Lord Jesus, you promise that everyone who keeps on asking will receive and those who keep on seeking will find you. When we knock, you will open the door for us. Keep us seeking you, Jesus. Open the door to us when we knock. Welcome us into your presence and supply our needs as you have promised. You promise that our heavenly Father will give us good gifts if we ask. We will list our needs and lay them before you. We are your children, and we are relying on you. Give us your perfect and good gifts. May we rejoice in your blessings to us and remember to thank you for all that you do for us.

GOD'S PROMISE TO YOU

- God opens the door to those who knock.
- He reveals himself to those who seek him.
- He gives good gifts to those who ask.

THE PROMISE
GOD IS GOOD

The Lord is kind and merciful, slow to get angry, full of unfailing love. The Lord is good to everyone. He showers compassion on all his creation. All of your works will thank you, Lord, and your faithful followers will bless you. They will talk together about the glory of your kingdom; they will celebrate examples of your power.   Psalm 145:8-11

Iт's all too easy to lapse into negativity, isn't it? It's so easy to complain. Our work demands are overwhelming. The housework is never completely finished. Our lives are too crowded with demands. If we're not careful, we can fall into the habit of talking about what's wrong instead of focusing on positive things.

King David, the author of Psalm 145, could have complained about a lot. He had a kingdom to run. He had enemies—people who were willing to take part in plots to overthrow him (Psalm 36:4). But in spite of all that David could have complained about, in this psalm he decided to focus on God's goodness to him and celebrate that. He knew God wants his people to give him thanks and praise and to tell others how good he is, how he saves those who come to him (Psalm 9:14). God wants people who will celebrate his goodness.

We can celebrate God every time we worship with other

believers, but we can also worship God in small ways every day—by stopping to rejoice in his creativity and beauty on display in our backyard garden or in the sky above. Learning to celebrate God's gifts each day will change your outlook on life. Ask God to help you and your spouse to look for his goodness in your marriage and in your daily lives. Pray today that your home and marriage will reflect God's power and love and celebrate his goodness.

PRAYING GOD'S PROMISE

Dear Lord, your Word promises that you are kind and merciful, slow to anger, and full of unfailing love. Thank you for being merciful to us. Show us your unfailing love and forgive our sins. Your Word tells us that you are good. We acknowledge your goodness. You have been so good to us. Remind us of your goodness often, and help us to celebrate it in our home.

GOD'S PROMISE TO YOU

- God is kind and merciful.
- He is slow to get angry and is full of unfailing love.
- He is good to everyone.

THE PROMISE
GOD GIVES US GIFTS FOR A PURPOSE

Cheerfully share your home with those who need a meal or a place to stay. God has given gifts to each of you from his great variety of spiritual gifts. Manage them well so that God's generosity can flow through you. Are you called to be a speaker? Then speak as though God himself were speaking through you. Are you called to help others? Do it with all the strength and energy that God supplies. Then God will be given glory in everything through Jesus Christ.   1 Peter 4:9-11

W HEN you come to God in prayer, does it often sound like a shopping list as you bring your needs to him? There's nothing wrong with expressing our needs and desires to God. He wants us to depend on him (Matthew 6:31-33). Yet we shouldn't simply look out for our own needs; we should be looking for ways we can meet the needs of others.

The Bible promises that God has given each of us special abilities and resources. But they're not just for our own enjoyment. He wants us to find opportunities to use these gifts in order to help others. He wants us to demonstrate his generosity to others through the gifts and abilities he has given us. There are a great variety of gifts. We don't need a special talent, such as singing or public speaking to share God's love with others. Your home or apartment—wherever you live—is also a gift from

God, and today's verses encourage us to share our home cheerfully. By sharing our resources and abilities with others, we're showing God's generosity to them. That pleases God, and he promises that he will supply strength and energy to those who expend themselves for him. As you pray today, ask God in what way he wants you to serve others, and then remember that God will supply the strength you need to do what he wants you to do.

PRAYING GOD'S PROMISE

Dear Lord, your Word promises that you have given spiritual gifts to each of us. Thank you for all of your good gifts, from our home to our interests and abilities. Help us to look for opportunities to use our gifts for your glory. We rely on your promise that you will give us the strength and energy we need to serve others with our gifts. Help us to create a home that encourages people to discover their gifts and use them to help others. We want to glorify you.

GOD'S PROMISE TO YOU

- God gives you spiritual gifts to use for his glory.
- He will give you the strength you need to use your gifts to serve others.

THE PROMISE
GOD GIVES US REST

Unless the Lord builds a house, the work of the builders is useless. Unless the Lord protects a city, guarding it with sentries will do no good. It is useless for you to work so hard from early morning until late at night, anxiously working for food to eat; for God gives rest to his loved ones.   Psalm 127:1-2

Do you ever feel as if your work and career goals rule your life? We get up before dawn and stay up late to meet deadlines. Time with our spouses and other family members gets squeezed out by work demands. We feel helpless to control the deluge of work. No matter what the situation is, the Bible encourages us to put work in its place—after devotion to God and our commitment to our marriages.

Work is a necessary part of life—it's even a gift from God!—but we need to keep it within its own time and place (Ecclesiastes 3:1, 9-13). God doesn't want us spending every hour thinking about work; he also wants us to spend time resting and enjoying his good gifts (Ecclesiastes 3:13). If you or your spouse is working too much—whether at the office or at home—ask God what you should do to change that. Do you need to set limits on how much time you will give to your work or talk with your employer about your priorities? Do you and your spouse need to talk about keeping each other accountable in holding to reasonable schedules? Do you need to look for a better work situation? Do you need to lower your career goals or your own expectations for yourself in order to have more time to rest? Ask God for guidance in balancing work with the rest of your life.

PRAYING GOD'S PROMISE

Dear Lord, your Word promises that any person or project connected to your purposes will last. We know our work is useless unless you bless it. Please give us wisdom to align our work responsibilities outside and inside the home to your will for us. Thank you for your gift of rest to the ones you love. Help us to see that as a good gift from you and to learn to take advantage of the rest you offer us. Renew and strengthen us as your Word promises you will.

GOD'S PROMISE TO YOU

- God gives rest to his loved ones.

THE PROMISE
GOD'S LOVE LASTS FOREVER

Our days on earth are like grass; like wildflowers, we bloom
and die. . . . But the love of the Lord remains forever with
those who fear him. His salvation extends to the children's children of those who are faithful to his covenant, of those who
obey his commandments!   Psalm 103:15-18

A wildflower sprouts up quickly after the spring rains. It
spreads out its pedals, displaying shades of bright oranges and
yellows. But when the heat of summer bears down on that
flower, it wilts and dies as quickly as it sprouted.

In today's verses David compares our human lives to those of
wildflowers. When we consider the great span of the history of
the cosmos, our eighty or even one hundred years on this earth
are short—very short. But the writer of Ecclesiastes says that
God has placed eternity in our hearts (3:11). We have a desire to
make a mark that lasts longer than our short life, and the only
way to create a lasting legacy is to participate in God's work
because only God and his work will last forever.

Scripture promises that if we consistently and faithfully obey
God we will leave a spiritual legacy to our children or to those
close to us (Psalm 112:1-4). What kind of spiritual legacy do you
want for your marriage? Pray that God will give you opportunities to share your faith with others. Pray that the relationship

154

that you and your spouse share will be a strong example to others of what a marriage can be. Ask God to help you make your home one that is characterized by faithfulness and obedience.

PRAYING GOD'S PROMISE

Dear Lord, you have told us that your love remains with us forever. We revere and respect you. Grant us eternal life so that we can enjoy your love, as your Word promises. Help us to build a home that encourages faithfulness to your commands so that we can leave a legacy of faith to the next generation.

GOD'S PROMISE TO YOU

- Life is short.
- God's love lasts forever for those who fear him.

THE PROMISE
GOD WILL ALWAYS GUIDE US

All I get is trouble all day long; every morning brings me pain.
. . . Yet I still belong to you; you are holding my right hand.
You will keep on guiding me with your counsel, leading me to
a glorious destiny. Whom have I in heaven but you? I desire
you more than anything on earth. My health may fail, and my
spirit may grow weak, but God remains the strength of my
heart; he is mine forever.   Psalm 73:14, 23-26

T H E key word in this psalm is "yet." Asaph, the writer, had lived
a long life and had seen much pain, misery, and evil. He even
described himself as envying the prosperity of the wicked
(Psalm 73:2-12). He had grown terribly bitter by everything he
had seen. "Yet I still belong to you; you are holding my right
hand," he proclaimed to God. Asaph realized how God had
helped him through the years to guard his heart and to keep his
life pure (Psalm 73:13). He saw how God kept on guiding him
day after day, year after year. God wouldn't abandon Asaph; he
would lead him to his glorious eternal destiny. Even when
Asaph felt weak, even when his health failed him, God was
there, strengthening and building him up.

Are there parts of your life that you're bitter about? Do you
find yourself tempted to envy the lives and homes of wicked
people? Decide today to echo Asaph's response: "Yet I still

belong to God." Pray that your home and your marriage will always belong to God and that God will remain the strength of your heart.

PRAYING GOD'S PROMISE

Dear Lord God, your Word promises that you will keep on guiding us. We see how people seem to prosper in spite of their wickedness and lack of integrity. Their lives seem so easy. Yet we still belong to you, oh God. Guide us with your counsel. Help us to love your truth and your laws. May our home and our marriage always belong to you. We know trouble will come and that at times we will feel weak. We are thankful for your promise that you will remain with us forever, providing the strength we need.

GOD'S PROMISE TO YOU

- God will keep on guiding you with his wise counsel.
- God will remain with you, giving you strength.

THE PROMISE
GOD GIVES US WHAT WE NEED

At the moment I have all I need—more than I need! I am generously supplied with the gifts you sent. . . . And this same God who takes care of me will supply all your needs from his glorious riches, which have been given to us in Christ Jesus.

Philippians 4:18-19

"At the moment I have all I need—more than I need!" Do these words sound as if they should be coming from a prisoner's mouth? When the apostle Paul penned them, he was under the watchful eyes of a palace guard (Philippians 1:13). But Paul was content with his circumstances because he kept his eyes on Jesus and on what Jesus wanted him to be and do (Philippians 3:12-14). Paul's life certainly wasn't easy. He had experienced hunger and thirst, insults and beatings (1 Corinthians 4:11-13). But he trusted that God would meet all of his needs. He committed his needs and the needs of those around him to God in prayer (Romans 1:9), and he asked God for the strength to endure the hardships that came his way.

We should have the same attitude Paul had. If we make God and his kingdom our first priority, God will take care of our needs (Matthew 6:31-33). So there's absolutely no reason to worry. The all-powerful God is in control of your life and your marriage. Your loving God, who has infinite riches, is able to take care of you (Psalm 145:15). What needs do you have today? As you pray, commit each one to God. Scripture promises that he will provide for you.

PRAYING GOD'S PROMISE

Dear God, your Word promises that you will supply everything we need. I commit my needs and the needs of my spouse to you. I know you are strong enough to protect us and rich enough to provide for us. Give us the confidence to trust that you love us and want only the best for us. Please take care of our needs so we can serve you wholeheartedly.

GOD'S PROMISE TO YOU

- God will give you everything you need.

THE PROMISE
GOD CARES FOR THOSE WHO ARE GENEROUS

All goes well for those who are generous, who lend freely and conduct their business fairly. Such people will not be overcome by evil circumstances. Those who are righteous will be long remembered. They do not fear bad news; they confidently trust the Lord to care for them. They are confident and fearless and can face their foes triumphantly. They give generously to those in need. Their good deeds will never be forgotten. They will have influence and honor.   Psalm 112:5-9

A spacious home. A well-paying job. A new car in the driveway. The luxuries that this world offers may appear to give the person who owns these things security and confidence. But Scripture says that placing our trust in money is a very dangerous thing to do. A well-paying job can disappear overnight. Stocks and mutual funds can decline. Another driver rear-ends the shiny new car. The only place we can securely and confidently place our trust is in God. We need to remember this when we're experiencing good times as well as bad times.

The Bible tells us that one way we can demonstrate our wholehearted trust in God is by giving away a portion of what we have. If we're generous with God first and our neighbors second, the Bible says, we won't have to "fear bad news" or "evil circumstances." Followers of God can be confident that he will take care of them. He is able to protect them and to supply all that they need. Ask God to create a generous spirit in your marriage. Look for opportunities to give generously to those in need, and ask God to cultivate a confident trust in him in your heart and home.

PRAYING GOD'S PROMISE

Dear Lord, your Word tells us that you will take care of those who are generous to others. Give us a generous spirit. Help us to want to give to those in need. Keep us from hoarding money, for we trust you will take care of us. Your Word promises that you inspire confidence in those who trust in you. We know we don't have to fear bad news because you are taking care of us. Build up our faith and our confidence in you, and free our home from fear.

GOD'S PROMISE TO YOU

- God takes care of those who are generous.
- He will inspire confidence in those who trust in him.

THE PROMISE
GOD DETERMINES OUR STEPS

Commit your work to the Lord, and then your plans will succeed. . . . We can make our plans, but the Lord determines our steps.   Proverbs 16:3, 9

I F you're like most couples, discussing your future together is one of your favorite pastimes. Where do you want to live? What kind of furniture would you like to buy? What kind of career or life goals do you want to pursue? If you're ambitious, you may even map out your dreams and goals. In fact, talking about your dreams and goals with your spouse can help each of you understand the other person better. And it provides a good opportunity to commit those dreams, desires, and goals to God.

Scripture promises that if you commit your work and plans to God, he will guide you and grant you success (Psalm 32:8). It doesn't, however, promise that everything will happen according to your well-laid plans. It's certainly good to make plans because they give you direction and a goal to work toward. But God will determine your steps. He knows the unplanned surprises that will come. He knows how you should react. Much more important than having well-laid plans is consistently following God every day. When you're doing that, you can trust him with the results. Then your home and marriage will rest securely on God's good plan for it.

PRAYING GOD'S PROMISE

Dear Lord, you are the One who gives the right answer, who allows plans to succeed, who determines our steps. We commit our thoughts, our work, and our plans to you. Thank you for determining our steps. Your Word promises that if we commit our work to you, you will grant us success. We dedicate today's work to you. Please grant your success to our efforts to build a solid marriage and a loving home.

GOD'S PROMISE TO YOU

- God wants you to commit your work and your plans to him.
- He determines the steps of his people.

THE PROMISE
JESUS IS OUR FRIEND

[Jesus said,] "Look! Here I stand at the door and knock. If you hear me calling and open the door, I will come in, and we will share a meal as friends. I will invite everyone who is victorious to sit with me on my throne, just as I was victorious and sat with my Father on his throne."   Revelation 3:20-21

C AN you think of a spot in your home—whether it's a closet or an entire room—in such disarray that you wouldn't want guests to see it? Visitors would be unwelcome there. You might keep the door shut and maybe even lock it if you could. If you have such a place, you probably wouldn't be comfortable with company getting close to it.

When it comes to our spiritual lives, we need to be careful that we don't lock Jesus out of our hearts and homes. Today's verses describe Jesus as standing at the door and knocking. He wants to enter every area of our lives, not just the ones we're comfortable with. Is there an area of your life where you have locked Jesus out? What is keeping you from accepting Jesus' great promise to eat with you and be your friend? Real friends are honest and open with each other, even when it's hard, because that's what real friendship looks like. Find time today to invite Jesus into every room of your home and every area of your life. As you pray, ask him to help you open the door in response to his call. Thank him for his promise to be your friend and your spouse's friend. Welcome him as the special guest in your home and your marriage. Ask God to help you make your home a place where Jesus will always feel welcome.

PRAYING GOD'S PROMISE

Dear Lord Jesus, you promise that if we hear you calling and open the door, you will share a meal with us as friends. Thank you, Jesus, for desiring to enter every part of our lives, for wanting to spend time with us. Keep us from shutting you out just because it makes us uncomfortable. Friends need to be honest and comfortable with each other. Be our powerful ally and friend. Help us to throw open the door to you and welcome you into each corner of our marriage so that our lives will honor you.

GOD'S PROMISE TO YOU

● God will be a friend to those who respond to his call.

THE PROMISE
GOD REWARDS THOSE WHO DO GOOD

[Jesus said,] "Love your enemies! Do good to them! Lend to them! And don't be concerned that they might not repay. Then your reward from heaven will be very great, and you will truly be acting as children of the Most High, for he is kind to the unthankful and to those who are wicked. You must be compassionate, just as your Father is compassionate. . . . If you give, you will receive. Your gift will return to you in full measure."

Luke 6:35-38

IT'S easy for us to be kind and compassionate when life is going fine. But what happens when difficult circumstances make our patience wear thin? What happens when those close to us start taking us for granted?

Scripture promises us that if we show kindness to those who are ungrateful, God will reward us. That's the kind of love he shows us. He loved us when we were still his enemies (Romans 5:6-8). He continues to give us our livelihood even when we forget to thank him (Luke 6:35). Jesus encourages us to show the same type of love to others. He wants us to give generously without expecting to be paid back. When we give to others with no strings attached, God is pleased. He sees what we are doing, and we can confidently expect him to give back to us much more than we give. We don't have to worry about whether others notice and acknowledge our acts of sacrifice or take us for granted. When we focus more on Christlike giving than on whether anyone notices our acts of kindness and sacrifice, we will be acting as God's children should. It's generous, Christlike love that keeps a home a welcoming and loving place.

PRAYING GOD'S PROMISE

Dear Lord, you are kind and compassionate to the ungrateful. You promise to reward those who do good to their enemies. Help us to be careful not to repay evil with evil. May we show compassion and kindness to those who are ungrateful, just as you do for us. Your Word promises that if we give to others, we will receive more back. Help us to think of others in forgiving and kind ways. Help us to joyously give to those in need. As we give, grant us your blessing on our home.

GOD'S PROMISE TO YOU

- God rewards those who do good to their enemies.
- He will give back in full measure to those who give to others.

THE PROMISE
GOD BLESSES THE GODLY

The Lord will not let the godly starve to death, but he refuses to satisfy the craving of the wicked. . . . The godly are showered with blessings; evil people cover up their harmful intentions. We all have happy memories of the godly, but the name of a wicked person rots away. Proverbs 10:3, 6-7

W H A T is your favorite memory? Memories are an important part of who you are. Your identity may be wrapped up in happy—or unhappy—childhood memories, memories of your first major accomplishment, or memories of your dating years with your spouse. Those memories settle in your mind, coloring how you see the world and react to it. What memories do you cherish? How do you cherish them? Through letters? photos? mementos? The writer of today's verses states a great truth: Happy memories are founded on godly living and God's blessing. The happiest memories are often those from a time when you were young or "innocent" and you embraced life with extraordinary gratitude for what God had given you. When you dedicate yourself to living according to God's truth, recognizing God's blessings, and completely trusting God's provision for all that you need, you're free to enjoy what God has given you. That sort of atmosphere can create an abundance of good memories for both you and others.

How do you want others to remember you? What kind of memories do you want to make for the people who enter your home? Ask God today to help you encourage godly living in your home so that your godly life will give others good memories of you.

PRAYING GOD'S PROMISE

Dear Lord, your Word tells us that you won't let the godly starve. You provide for the needs of your people. We are depending on you to provide what we need. Help us to live godly lives so that we can enjoy your blessings. We are your people. We are following you. Help us to live in a way that will create happy memories for others.

GOD'S PROMISE TO YOU

- Godly people know God's blessings.
- Godly people provide happy memories for others.

THE PROMISE
GOD MAKES US FRUITFUL

Then God said, "Let us make people in our image, to be like ourselves. They will be masters over all life—the fish in the sea, the birds in the sky, and all the livestock, wild animals, and small animals." So God created people in his own image; God patterned them after himself; male and female he created them. God blessed them and told them, "Multiply and fill the earth and subdue it." . . . God looked over all he had made, and he saw that it was excellent in every way.   Genesis 1:26-28, 31

CONTRARY to what some people believe, marriage isn't a necessary evil resulting from humankind's fallenness. From the beginning all that God had created was "excellent in every way." In fact, men and women together reflect God's image.

In what ways do we reflect God's image? First, we were created for relationship, as male and female. When God refers to his creating us in his own image, he uses plural pronouns, "our image" and "ourselves," an indication of his plural nature as God the Father, God the Son, and God the Holy Spirit. Human beings reflect God's plural nature because he created both male and female. Just as God the Son and God the Father enjoy relationship (Hebrews 5:7), men and women are created for relationship (Genesis 2:18). Most important, loving marriage relationships between men and women reflect Christ's love for the church (Ephesians 5:25-30).

Second, men and women reflect God's image when they rule over this world. When we take care of the world God has given us, we're reflecting God's rule over the universe.

Third, God blessed men and women and told them to multiply. This ability to multiply reflects God's own creative nature. For some people this blessing translates into children entrusted to their care (Psalm 128:3-4). Couples who don't have children participate in this blessing when they multiply their spiritual legacy in the hearts of other people—their spiritual children—just as the apostle Paul did (1 Thessalonians 1:6-7). Are your home and marriage reflecting God's image in loving and fruitful ways? Ask God to help you do that.

PRAYING GOD'S PROMISE

Dear Lord, you created us in your own image, and you created marriage as your gift to us. Please bless our marriage union. Empower us to reflect your image accurately. Bless our home, and make it fruitful for your glory.

GOD'S PROMISE TO YOU

- God created men and women in his image.
- He created marriage as a gift.
- He wants your marriage to reflect Christ's love.

THE PROMISE
GOD CARES FOR US

[Jesus said,] "Why worry about your clothes? Look at the lilies and how they grow. They don't work or make their clothing, yet Solomon in all his glory was not dressed as beautifully as they are. And if God cares so wonderfully for flowers that are here today and gone tomorrow, won't he more surely care for you? You have so little faith!"   Matthew 6:28-30

I F we're not careful, worry can take over our lives. There are so many things we can't control. We wonder, *Is my spouse safe? Will my job remain secure? Will the car continue to run?* Then we look beyond our homes to our communities, our nation, and the world, and so many pressing needs come to mind—food for the hungry, supplies for war-torn nations, and assistance to refugees. It can quickly become overwhelming. But in today's verses Jesus gives us an extraordinary glimpse into the mind of God. To paraphrase Jesus' words, God is asking, "Why do my people worry? I am the Creator of the entire world—the stately mountains, the fruitful plains, and the sparkling streams. I take care of the most insignificant wildflower. These are all signs of my continuing care for the world my people live in. Why don't they trust me with their needs?"

Take a few minutes today to adjust your perspective on your worries and troubles. What blessings from God are you currently enjoying? How has God shown again and again that he will provide for you and your spouse? God is willing and able to take care of you. The next time you begin to have doubts and give in to worry, remind yourself of today's promise from the Bible, and think about all the ways God has cared for you in the past. When you do, you'll be reminded that there really isn't any reason to worry (Luke 12:22-25). Ask God to help you trust his faithfulness more and more.

PRAYING GOD'S PROMISE

Dear Jesus, your Word promises that we don't need to worry, that we can confidently trust God for what we need. We lay our worries before you, and we resolve with your help to trust you whole-heartedly. You have shown us that you care for us; you clothe us, feed us, and provide shelter for us. Thank you for your faithfulness in attending to all our needs. From our greatest needs to our smallest, you, oh God, are our great provider.

GOD'S PROMISE TO YOU

- God will take care of your needs.

THE PROMISE
GOD WASHES US CLEAN

Have mercy on me, O God, because of your unfailing love.
Because of your great compassion, blot out the stain of my sins.
Wash me clean from my guilt. Purify me from my sin. . . . You
desire honesty from the heart, so you can teach me to be wise
in my inmost being. Purify me from my sins, and I will be
clean; wash me, and I will be whiter than snow. Oh, give me
back my joy again.   Psalm 51:1-2, 6-8

K ING David wrote this psalm after the prophet Nathan told
him that God would punish him for his adulterous affair with
Bathsheba and for arranging the murder of Bathsheba's
husband, Uriah. King David had clearly sinned against God and
the nation. Why then did God call David "a man after my own
heart" (Acts 13:22)? Psalm 51 gives us the answer. David sought
God throughout his life. When he realized he had sinned, he
humbled himself before God, confessed his sin, and asked God
for mercy. Even after such serious sins as adultery and murder,
David didn't give in to despair and give up. He knew God was
bigger than his sins. He knew God's mercy was greater than his
rebellion. But David also understood that God cannot stand
the filth of sin. God is holy, and he wants purity and honesty in
our inmost being.

David couldn't clean the sin from his soul. But God could.

God could wash David clean and give back to him the joy of living in harmony with his Creator. The Bible promises that God will wash clean those who turn to him for forgiveness (1 John 1:9). If God is willing to forgive our darkest sins, we need to be willing to show forgiveness to our spouses (Colossians 3:13). Ask God to help you create a joy-filled home by showing Christlike forgiveness to those who live there and those who enter it.

PRAYING GOD'S PROMISE

Dear God, you will forgive our sins because of your unfailing love and compassion. You promise to wash us whiter than snow and give us back genuine joy when we are honest with you about our sins. We want to be clean. Forgive our sins, and help us to show forgiveness to each other. Your Word promises that when we are honest with you, you will teach us to be wise in our inmost being. Help us to be honest about our sins, and teach us to be wise so that we can live rightly and have your joy.

GOD'S PROMISE TO YOU

- God shows you mercy because of his unfailing love.
- Because of his compassion, he will blot out the stain of your sin.
- God will teach you wisdom and restore his joy to you.

THE PROMISE
GOD BLESSES THOSE WHO ENDURE

Dear brothers and sisters, whenever trouble comes your way, let it be an opportunity for joy. For when your faith is tested, your endurance has a chance to grow. So let it grow, for when your endurance is fully developed, you will be strong in character and ready for anything. . . . God blesses the people who patiently endure testing. Afterward they will receive the crown of life that God has promised to those who love him.

James 1:2-4, 12

WHAT color were your glasses on your wedding day? Many times the happy couple is wearing rose-colored glasses. A brand-new husband or wife can appear to be perfect on that wonderful day. A happy future together lies before you, and you feel as if nothing can ever go wrong.

Then things do start to go wrong. Large unexpected plumbing bills need to be paid. The car doesn't work quite right. The house needs repairs. Now life isn't looking quite so rosy. In a few years even bigger troubles come—family problems, disagreements with your neighbors, conflict at work, conflict in your marriage. You soon find out that what the Bible says is true: life is filled with troubles (Psalm 88:3).

As Christians we can expect conflict with the people of this world because they don't understand the truth (John 15:20). So it's not a question of whether we will have troubles, it's only a question of how we will handle them. The Bible promises that God will reward those who patiently endure testing, difficulties, and troubles. When situations are difficult, our character and faith are put to the test. And when with God's help and strength we pass those tests, we're stronger.

Pray today that God will give you and your spouse the patience to endure the troubles you will face in your marriage. Ask him to help you develop a faith that doesn't panic about troubles but instead sees them as opportunities for growth and joy.

PRAYING GOD'S PROMISE

Dear Lord, the Bible promises that you bless people who patiently endure testing. It promises that our character will grow stronger when we endure troubles. Help us to find joy in the midst of our troubles. Point out to us what you're trying to develop in our character. Keep us faithful in times of trouble so that one day we will receive the blessing you have for those who endure. Help us to keep our eyes on the crown of life that you have promised for those who patiently accept testing and don't give up.

GOD'S PROMISE TO YOU

- God allows troubles in your life to build your character and your faith.
- He will bless you if you patiently endure testing.
- Those who love God will inherit a crown of life.

THE PROMISE
GOD DRAWS CLOSE TO THOSE
WHO DRAW CLOSE TO HIM

Humble yourselves before God. Resist the Devil, and he will flee from you. Draw close to God, and God will draw close to you. . . . Let there be tears for the wrong things you have done. Let there be sorrow and deep grief. Let there be sadness instead of laughter, and gloom instead of joy. When you bow down before the Lord and admit your dependence on him, he will lift you up and give you honor.   James 4:7-10

T HERE are times when tears are more appropriate than laughter, sorrow more appropriate than rejoicing (Ecclesiastes 7:3). When sorrow leads you to turn from sin and ask God to change your heart, sorrow is actually life-giving. Jesus promises that God will bless those who mourn over their sin; he will rescue those who humble themselves before him (Matthew 5:4). It's good to spend time reflecting on your marriage and life, praying that God will change you according to his holy and perfect will. Today's verses say that if you set aside time to draw close to God, he will draw close to you. Those who seek God will find him (Matthew 7:7). Today's passage in James may not sound entirely comforting. But in reality it holds one of the greatest promises: If we humble ourselves before God and turn from our sins, God will respond. He won't let us languish where we are.

He will rescue us and lift us up when we admit our dependence on him. He will give us his Spirit's power within us so that when we resist the devil and his temptations, he will flee from us.

Pray today that your home will be an example to others of what humility before God and dependence on him look like.

PRAYING GOD'S PROMISE

Dear Lord, your Word promises that if we humble ourselves before you and resist the devil, he will flee from us. Help us to resist the temptations of the evil one. Keep evil from gaining a foothold in our home. You have promised that if we draw close to you, you will draw close to us; if we bow before you, you will lift us up. We want our marriage to reflect our intimacy with you. Help us always to demonstrate humility with each other and with you. Lift us up as your Word promises.

GOD'S PROMISE TO YOU

- God lifts up those who humbly bow before him.
- He honors those who admit their dependence on him.

THE PROMISE
GOD HONORS THE HUMBLE

Two men went to the Temple to pray. One was a Pharisee, and the other was a dishonest tax collector. The proud Pharisee . . . prayed this prayer: "I thank you, God, that I am not a sinner like everyone else, especially like that tax collector over there! For I never cheat, I don't sin, I don't commit adultery, I fast twice a week, and I give you a tenth of my income." But the tax collector . . . beat his chest in sorrow, saying, "O God, be merciful to me, for I am a sinner." . . . The proud will be humbled, but the humble will be honored.   Luke 18:10-14

I n this passage Jesus paints a picture of two different ways to approach God in prayer. One man, a Pharisee, was among the most respected people in his community. He ordered his life according to the most exacting standards of that day—and he knew it. He prayed to God because it was his duty, but he didn't really think he needed God. Prayer was simply an exercise. The other man, a dishonest tax collector, understood all too well that he was a sinner. He knew without a doubt that he needed God's mercy. He also knew that he didn't deserve it.

Whom did God listen to? The tax collector. Why? Because he had humbled himself before God. Do you ever find your times of prayer becoming routine? Take some time today to meditate on what a privilege you have to be able to approach God in prayer. Admit your sins before him, and ask him to show you how to walk in humility before him. After you have humbled yourself, you can ask him to honor you and your home. Scripture promises that God will honor those who come to him in humility (1 Peter 5:6).

PRAYING GOD'S PROMISE

Dear Jesus, your Word promises that you will show mercy to those who humble themselves before you. We humble ourselves now, oh God, and acknowledge that we are sinners in need of your mercy. Please show mercy to us. You promise that the humble will be honored. We pray that you will keep us from growing proud. Help us to learn genuine humility so that we can receive your honor as you have said.

GOD'S PROMISE TO YOU

- God will honor you when you humble yourself before him.

THE PROMISE
GOD IS OUR EXAMPLE

Get rid of all bitterness, rage, anger, harsh words, and slander,
as well as all types of malicious behavior. Instead, be kind to
each other, tenderhearted, forgiving one another, just as God
through Christ has forgiven you. Follow God's example in
everything you do, because you are his dear children. Live a
life filled with love for others, following the example of Christ,
who loved you and gave himself as a sacrifice to take away
your sins.   Ephesians 4:31–5:2

WE'VE all seen a girl imitating her mother—cooking, putting on
makeup, and so on. Boys often mimic their father's gestures or
tone of voice. When children are young, these efforts to do what
their parents do are often obvious and humorous. Later on,
when these same children grow up, they may continue to follow
their parents' example, but by then it's less obvious. In today's
passage the apostle Paul encourages us to follow the example of
our spiritual Father in heaven. We are to follow God's example
in everything we do. We are to love the way Jesus loved us. We
are to be kind and forgiving just as Jesus forgave us and showed
us loving-kindness (Matthew 6:12).

Doing this day in and day out is difficult. Conflicts arise, and
our selfish natures make it easy to lash out in anger and cultivate an attitude of bitterness. Often it's in our home that we

show our worst sides. Pray today that you will be able to follow God's example, being kind and forgiving and sacrificial toward others. Ask God to help you to be tenderhearted and to speak words of love and encouragement to your spouse. As you do those things, you will be following your heavenly Father's example.

PRAYING GOD'S PROMISE

Dear God, your Word promises that you will forgive us and save us. Thank you for identifying us as your own and for being our example. Help us not to bring sorrow to the Holy Spirit by the way we live. Help us to resist the temptation to use harsh words or to have an unforgiving attitude. We are your children because Jesus Christ sacrificed himself to pay for our sins. Thank you for making us your children. Help us to follow Christ's example in all we do and say.

GOD'S PROMISE TO YOU

- God has made you his child because of Jesus' sacrifice.
- You are to forgive others in the same way that God has forgiven you.

THE PROMISE
GOD HEALS THE BROKENHEARTED

[God] heals the brokenhearted, binding up their wounds. He counts the stars and calls them all by name. How great is our Lord! His power is absolute! His understanding is beyond comprehension! . . . The Lord's delight is in those who honor him, those who put their hope in his unfailing love.

Psalm 147:3-5, 11

WHY does God care so much about us? The God we worship made the entire universe. He can call every one of the stars in the cosmos by name. The entire world is at his command (Psalm 147:15). He causes the rain to fall. He makes certain the green grass grows over the rolling hills and mountain pastures (Psalm 147:8). He provides food for the raven and sparrow, the deer and bear (Psalm 147:9). He holds our world and all of creation in his mighty hand. Yet he is also concerned about you, about the condition of your heart (Psalm 44:21). He sees its wounds—the hidden hurts that only you can feel. God knows what it's like to be weak and brokenhearted because Jesus experienced those things on earth (Hebrews 4:14-16).

God wants to heal your inner hurts. Although God can direct his attention to anything in the universe—the majesty of the mountains, the bright vast seas, the sparkling stars above—the Bible says that he takes delight in those whose hearts are devoted to him. He delights in those who honor him and place their hope in him (Deuteronomy 30:10). He takes delight in you.

Take time today to open your heart to God, admitting your hurts and giving him your brokenness. Ask him to heal any inner hurts of your spouse as well. Then recommit your heart, your life, your spouse, and your marriage to God's glory and honor.

PRAYING GOD'S PROMISE

Dear God, your Word promises that you heal the brokenhearted and bind up their wounds. You are great, oh Lord. You know not only every star above but also the wounds in my heart. Please heal those wounds as you have promised. You delight in those who honor you, those who put their hope in your love. We honor you. Your unfailing love is our only hope. We pray that you will take delight in us and in our marriage.

GOD'S PROMISE TO YOU

- God can heal your broken heart and bind up your wounds.
- He delights in those who honor him.
- He delights in those who put their hope in his unfailing love.

THE PROMISE
GOD BLESSES OUR HOME

Do not envy violent people; don't copy their ways. Such wicked people are an abomination to the Lord, but he offers his friendship to the godly. The curse of the Lord is on the house of the wicked, but his blessing is on the home of the upright. The Lord mocks at mockers, but he shows favor to the humble.

Proverbs 3:31-34

SOMETIMES the lifestyles of evil people seem alluring. Why is gangsta rap so popular? Those music stars have it all—power, wealth, and fame. Often, the more they flout social norms and God's law, the more popular and wealthy they become. People who seek fame and wealth by ignoring God's law may appear to be extraordinarily successful for a while. But the Bible says their success will quickly evaporate, for God's blessing isn't on them (Proverbs 10:29-30).

Violent people will meet a violent end (Psalm 140:11). Greedy people will lose the money they hoarded (Luke 12:15-21). And God will mock those who mock him. But those who seek God will gain eternal rewards. Not only will they have an eternal inheritance that will never fade, but they will also enjoy God's blessing and protection in this life. When disaster strikes, they won't have to fear because God is their friend. His favor rests on their home. The lives of the wicked may be exciting or flashy, but they are filled with heartache and disappointment and wasted years.

The writer of Proverbs presents us with a choice. We can copy the ways of the wicked and waste our lives, or we can copy God's way and know his blessing now and enjoy eternal treasures from the hand of God (Matthew 6:19-21). Which way will you choose for your household?

PRAYING GOD'S PROMISE

Dear Lord, your Word says that you offer friendship to the godly. We want to follow your ways. We want a deep friendship with you. Help us to live uprightly and to build our home on your principles so that we will know your blessing on our marriage and home.

GOD'S PROMISE TO YOU

- God is the friend of those who are godly.
- He will bless your home if you live uprightly.
- He will show his favor to those who are humble.

THE PROMISE
GOD'S SPIRIT REVEALS GOD'S SECRETS

The Scriptures . . . say, "No eye has seen, no ear has heard, and no mind has imagined what God has prepared for those who love him." But we know these things because God has revealed them to us by his Spirit, and his Spirit searches out everything and shows us even God's deep secrets. No one can know what anyone else is really thinking except that person alone, and no one can know God's thoughts except God's own Spirit. And God has actually given us his Spirit (not the world's spirit) so we can know the wonderful things God has freely given us.   1 Corinthians 2:9-12

T HE most difficult obstacle in cultivating a marriage devoted to God is our tendency to become distracted by the world. No matter who we are, we are influenced by what other people think is important. What this world values—wealth and fame, power and success—affects the way we think and the decisions we make. That is why it's so important that we counteract the values of the world by regularly reading and studying the Bible. We need to know the true values in God's Word to correct the values we absorb from our culture.

The Bible promises us that God has planted his Spirit, not the world's spirit, in our hearts to help us understand what God values (John 14:26). God's Spirit redirects our hearts away from the world and toward God. In doing so, he enables us to claim all of God's wonderful promises because those good promises are for those who love and follow God. Because the Spirit is within us, we can begin to understand all the wonderful things God has freely given us (1 Corinthians 2:12). So, in a way, the promise of God's Spirit within us unlocks many other Bible promises for us.

When you notice the world's values seeping into your home, ask God's Spirit to help you reorient your marriage around God's ways. Pray that God's Spirit will guide you and your spouse and help you to understand the wonderful things God is preparing for you.

PRAYING GOD'S PROMISE

Dear God, your Word promises that you are preparing great things for those who love you. We love you, and we want to see those great things you are preparing. In the meantime, may we be content with your plan for our lives and marriages. Thank you for planting your Spirit in our hearts to keep us turned toward you and to reveal the wonderful things you have given us.

GOD'S PROMISE TO YOU

- God is preparing great things for those who love him.
- God has given his Spirit to you to reveal his wonderful plan for you.

THE PROMISE
GOD GUIDES US

The Lord says, "I will guide you along the best pathway for your life. I will advise you and watch over you.". . . Many sorrows come to the wicked, but unfailing love surrounds those who trust the Lord. So rejoice in the Lord and be glad, all you who obey him! Shout for joy, all you whose hearts are pure!

Psalm 32:8-11

Do you remember the last major decision you made about some aspect of your life? Was it a choice about your career? your education? the amount of time you spend with your children? Before you arrived at your decision, you may have asked many people for advice. The Bible says that there is value in gaining good counsel from others, but the most important person you can ask for advice is God. Today's verses promise that God will counsel you and watch over you. He promises to lead you along the very best pathway for your life if you submit to his direction.

God is glad to guide you when you are facing big decisions, but he wants you to seek his guidance when the decisions you face aren't so big. Nothing in your life is too small to take to God. He wants you to look to him daily for guidance (Psalm 5:3). When you place your trust in God on a daily basis, you will be surrounded by his unfailing love and you will know his peace. Each step of the way, you will feel God's loving and guiding hand.

Ask God in prayer today to guide you, your home life, and your marriage along the best pathway. Pray that he will help you to seek his guidance in everything.

PRAYING GOD'S PROMISE

Dear God, you promise to guide us along the best pathway, and you tell us that your unfailing love will surround those who trust in you. Thank you for loving us enough to care what pathway we take. Guide us every day in our marriage. We ask you to advise and watch over us. We want to know the joy that you give to those who love you and obey you. Please watch over my spouse and my home. Direct us in all our decisions, big and small, and help us to go where you lead.

GOD'S PROMISE TO YOU

- God will guide you along the best path.
- He will advise you and watch over you.
- His unfailing love will surround you as you trust him.

PART 4

PRAYING FOR GOD TO BE AT THE CENTER OF OUR MARRIAGE

O n the day when you said, "I do," God was there. He witnessed your marriage vows to each other (Malachi 2:14). You weren't simply making a promise in front of your relatives and friends, your mother and father. You were making them in the presence of God, and he heard those vows. On that memorable day, God made the two of you one (Mark 10:8-9). So from the start, whether you were aware of it or not, God was there.

It's difficult to keep God at the center of our marriage relationships every day. We can do that by dedicating our marriages to God. We can do it by studying the Bible and making certain that we're living according to God's ways (1 Peter 1:15). We can invite God to be the center of our marriages by praying together with our spouses (Colossians 4:2).

When God is at the center of our marriages, we can ask him to guide and direct us. God will bless us and will strengthen our love for each other (Proverbs 3:33). When we make God our first priority, everything else in our lives will find its proper place (Matthew 6:33).

THE PROMISE
GOD GRANTS SUCCESS

[The Lord said to Joshua,] "Be strong and very courageous. Obey all the laws Moses gave you. Do not turn away from them, and you will be successful in everything you do. Study this Book of the Law continually. Meditate on it day and night so you may be sure to obey all that is written in it. Only then will you succeed. I command you—be strong and courageous! Do not be afraid or discouraged. For the Lord your God is with you wherever you go."   Joshua 1:7-9

W HAT a promise God gave Joshua! If Joshua would be careful to obey God's laws, God would grant him success. Joshua wouldn't have to fear, for he would know God was always with him and was working through him. We can rely on similar promises if we believe in Jesus and follow God's ways (John 15:5-8).

The Bible says that if we fear and respect God, we will succeed (Ecclesiastes 7:18). Why is that? Because instead of chasing our own goals and desires, instead of building our own empires and castles, we will be working for God's kingdom. Our efforts will be aligned with what God wants to accomplish in us and in the world. When that happens, we can be assured of success because God is in our work. Success may not come quickly, and it may not be success according to the world's standards. There may even be many failures along the way. But God assures us that in the end our efforts won't be fruitless. Our work will have eternal value, and it will bear eternal fruit because we're working for God. If we commit our work and marriage to God, God will grant success in his own time and in his own way (Proverbs 16:3). When we are successful, we need to be careful to say, as the apostle Paul did, "Our only power and success come from God" (2 Corinthians 3:5).

PRAYING GOD'S PROMISE

Dear Lord, you promise success to those who obey you. Thank you for giving us your Word so that we can know you and discover your will for us. Help us to obey you. We want to be successful in your eyes. You promised to be with Joshua wherever he would go. We want you to be with us, and we want to follow you all of our days. Keep us from discouragement, and grant us strength and courage to follow you wherever you lead us.

GOD'S PROMISE TO YOU

- God will bless you as you obey him.
- He is with you wherever you go.

THE PROMISE
GOD REWARDS THOSE WHO SEEK HIM

It is impossible to please God without faith. Anyone who wants
to come to him must believe that there is a God and that he
rewards those who sincerely seek him. . . . All these faithful
ones died without receiving what God had promised them, but
they saw it all from a distance and welcomed the promises of
God. They agreed that they were no more than foreigners and
nomads here on earth. . . .They were looking for a better place,
a heavenly homeland. That is why God is not ashamed to be
called their God, for he has prepared a heavenly city for them.

Hebrews 11:6, 13, 16

WHEN we approach God in prayer, we must have faith. We must
believe that God is listening and loves us enough to answer our
prayers. What is this faith that we must have? The author of
Hebrews explains that "it is the confident assurance that what
we hope for is going to happen. It is the evidence of things we
cannot yet see" (Hebrews 11:1). This faith that we need when
we approach God is a gift he gives to us, and it's good that he
does because we can't please him without it (Ephesians 2:8).

Just like God's faithful followers in the past, we welcome
many of God's promises from a distance. Abraham confidently
believed God's promise that his descendants would inherit the
Promised Land even though he remained a foreigner. In the

same way, we have confidence that one day Jesus will return to rule over all (1 Corinthians 15:24-28). Like Abraham, we may die without receiving all of God's promises, but that doesn't mean they aren't true. God will fulfill them in ways and times we can't imagine, in the eternal home he is creating for us (John 14:1-4). When we don't see some of God's promises being fulfilled in our lives, we should ask God for a more long-term perspective. The God we worship is eternal, and none of his promises will fail. He is as good as his word.

PRAYING GOD'S PROMISE

Dear Lord, your Word promises that you will reward those who seek you. We believe that you exist and that you reward those who genuinely seek you. We have placed our faith in you. We look forward to the reward you have promised your children. The Bible promises that you are not ashamed to be called our God and that you are preparing a heavenly home for us. We're nomads on this earth, and we're looking for a better place—the heavenly home to which you have called us. Keep our hearts fixed on you and on our eternal home as we await the fulfillment of your promises.

GOD'S PROMISE TO YOU

- You cannot please God without faith.
- God is preparing a heavenly home for those who believe in him.

THE PROMISE
GOD IS WORKING IN US

Your attitude should be the same that Christ Jesus had. Though he was God, he did not demand and cling to his rights as God. He made himself nothing; he took the humble position of a slave and . . . in human form he obediently humbled himself even further by dying a criminal's death on a cross. . . . Put into action God's saving work in your lives, obeying God with deep reverence and fear. For God is working in you, giving you the desire to obey him and the power to do what pleases him.

Philippians 2:5-8, 12-13

W HAT would happen if a wealthy CEO gave up his wealth and power to take a low-paying service job? The press would report it, and people would discuss it in disbelief. It's natural for people to work to gain wealth and power. It's extremely rare for people to give it up once they have it. But that is exactly what Jesus did for us on an immeasurably grander scale. He voluntarily set aside the privileges he enjoyed in heaven with his Father to become a lowly human being and to die as the sacrifice for our sins (Romans 8:1-4).

The Bible calls those who believe in Jesus to the same type of humble obedience. We are God's servants, and we should be willing to serve him in any position and in any place (Romans 6:22). If we have wealth or abilities or a position of influence,

God has given them to us to use in serving him. It's difficult to follow in Christ's footsteps. But the Bible says the Holy Spirit is working within you, convicting you of the truth and giving you the desire to obey. Isn't that amazing? God recreates your heart and mind so that you can love and obey him (2 Corinthians 5:17). When you struggle in moments of weakness, this precious promise can give you hope. Following Christ is not all up to you.

PRAYING GOD'S PROMISE

Dear Jesus, although you obediently humbled yourself to die on the cross for us, the Bible promises that one day everyone will bow before you. We bow before you now. Cultivate in us a Christlike humility and a willingness to follow in your footsteps. Keep us from sin and give us the desire and the power to obey you so that our lives will honor you.

GOD'S PROMISE TO YOU

- One day everyone will bow before Jesus.
- God will give you the desire to obey him.

THE PROMISE
GOD WILL RESCUE THOSE WHO TRUST HIM

[God said,] "All the animals of the forest are mine, and I own the cattle on a thousand hills. Every bird of the mountains and all the animals of the field belong to me. If I were hungry, I would not mention it to you, for all the world is mine and everything in it. I don't need the bulls you sacrifice; I don't need the blood of goats. What I want instead is your true thanks to God; I want you to fulfill your vows to the Most High. Trust me in your times of trouble, and I will rescue you, and you will give me glory." Psalm 50:10-15

WHAT'S the most important thing we can do on Sunday at church? Is it teaching Sunday school? Taking care of children in the nursery? Is it serving coffee after church? All these things are important. But we need to remind ourselves that the reason we come to church is to worship God and give him glory. We come to thank God for showering his good gifts on us during another week. We should commit our lives and time to serving God, but God doesn't need our service and our sacrifice. He owns the entire world and could accomplish his purposes without us if he wanted to, but he chooses to work through us because he loves us. What he wants from us is our praise and thanks and the glory he so richly deserves. He wants our worship more than anything else.

When troubles rock your home and your marriage, don't forget to worship God in the midst of your difficulties. When you are trusting him, he is working to rescue you. When you see his hand at work, thank him for his involvement in your life. Remind yourself to tell others the marvelous things God has done for you. God loves to receive your honor and glory and heartfelt thanks.

PRAYING GOD'S PROMISE

Dear Creator God, everything on earth is yours. You don't need anything from us. But you desire our genuine thanks for everything you've given us. Thank you for all you have given us. We know that every good thing we have in our marriage is from you. You promise that you will rescue those who trust you in times of trouble. We place our wholehearted trust in you. We give you our troubles and trust you to rescue us. May we recognize the way you are working on our behalf and give you the glory you deserve.

GOD'S PROMISE TO YOU

- God will rescue you when you trust him in times of trouble.

THE PROMISE
GOD MAKES OUR PATH SMOOTH

You will keep in perfect peace all who trust in you, whose thoughts are fixed on you! Trust in the Lord always, for the Lord God is the eternal Rock. . . . But for those who are righteous, the path is not steep and rough. You are a God of justice, and you smooth out the road ahead of them. Lord, we love to obey your laws; our heart's desire is to glorify your name. All night long I search for you; earnestly I seek for God.

Isaiah 26:3-4, 7-9

IF you have ever watched or participated in a marathon, you've heard the sounds of feet hitting the pavement—*Plop. Plop. Plop.* At the start of the race the path is level and the pace is quick. But as the hours drag on and the path becomes steep and rough, the pace slows dramatically.

Life is like a marathon. Sometimes the path is easy and the pace quick. At other times the path becomes steep, fatigue slows your pace, and you feel like giving up. The Bible promises that if you fix your thoughts on God, he will give you the strength you need to finish the race (Philippians 3:12-21). Today's verses say that as you follow the path of righteousness, God will smooth out the road ahead of you. That doesn't mean you will never experience difficulties and troubles and rough roads, but it does mean that God is with you and will help you.

If your heart's desire is to glorify God and obey his laws, you can trust him to see you through any problem and difficulty. When you and your spouse encounter bumps in the road, commit them to God. Ask him to guide you through the rough times and to give each of you strength to keep running on his path for your marriage. When you keep your thoughts fixed on the goal ahead—finishing the race and glorifying God—he will give you his peace.

PRAYING GOD'S PROMISE

Dear God, your Word promises that you will keep in perfect peace those who trust in you. You are the eternal Rock, in whom we can confidently place our trust. We do trust you, oh God. Please help us to trust you more. Give us your perfect peace about what we're doing and where we're going. Thank you for your promise to smooth out the path of those who are righteous. Protect us from slipping and falling, and give us your strength so that we can stay on the path. Guide us in your righteous ways.

GOD'S PROMISE TO YOU

- God will give you his perfect peace when you trust him.
- He will smooth out your path if you are living righteously.

THE PROMISE
GOD TAKES MARRIAGE SERIOUSLY

> You cover the Lord's altar with tears, weeping and groaning because he pays no attention to your offerings, and he doesn't accept them with pleasure. You cry out, "Why has the Lord abandoned us?" I'll tell you why! Because the Lord witnessed the vows you and your wife made to each other on your wedding day when you were young. But you have been disloyal to her, though she remained your faithful companion, the wife of your marriage vows. Malachi 2:13-14

"GOD loves you deeply." That was the message the prophet Malachi had for the people of his day (Malachi 1:2). His hearers had much evidence of God's love for them. He had brought them back from exile in the wicked land of Babylon in order to resettle the land of Judah, rebuild the temple in Jerusalem, and reestablish their families in the land. But still they doubted God's love. They even thought God had abandoned them. Why wasn't God paying attention to their offerings? Because they had not been faithful to their spouses. They had broken their wedding vows and married other people who weren't dedicated to God (Malachi 2:11). God had heard their vows in their youth and expected them to keep the commitments they had made to each other, but they had failed to do so. That's why God wasn't taking note of their sacrifices.

God takes marriage very seriously. It is his desire that spouses remain faithful to each other (Proverbs 5:18). He loves it when marriages reflect God's faithful love for his people. But it grieves him so much when vows are broken that later in chapter 2 of Malachi he says, "I hate divorce! It is as cruel as putting on a victim's bloodstained coat." God knows the pain and damage that occur when one or both partners break their commitment to each other. As you pray today, commit your marriage and your spouse to God. Ask him to guard your marriage and keep your hearts faithful to each other.

PRAYING GOD'S PROMISE

Dear God, we read in your Word that you make a husband and wife one. Protect me from anything that may tempt me to be disloyal to my spouse. Help me to remain faithful to my marriage vows so that nothing will be able to break the bond that you have given us. Keep us close to you and close to each other so that our faithfulness to our marriage vows will reflect your faithfulness to those you love.

GOD'S PROMISE TO YOU

• God desires that husbands and wives keep their commitment to each other.

THE PROMISE
JESUS GIVES US ACCESS TO GOD IN PRAYER

[Jesus said,] "The words I say are not my own, but my Father who lives in me does his work through me. Just believe that I am in the Father and the Father is in me. Or at least believe because of what you have seen me do. The truth is, anyone who believes in me will do the same works I have done, and even greater works, because I am going to be with the Father. You can ask for anything in my name, and I will do it, because the work of the Son brings glory to the Father."

John 14:10-13

TODAY's passage is Jesus' answer to Philip's request: "Lord, show us the Father and we will be satisfied" (John 14:8). Philip was looking for God the Father, and Jesus redirected Philip's search with his response. We can know what God is like because of what Jesus said and did when he was on earth. We can know God the Father by looking at Jesus because Jesus is in the Father and the Father is in Jesus. Jesus translated this mystery into a wonderful promise concerning prayer: *Ask in Jesus' name, and Jesus will do it because his work is God's work.* When Jesus left the earth and went to God the Father, Jesus opened a direct line of communication to God. Believers in Jesus can pray directly to God, in Jesus' name (Hebrews 10:21-22). The Israelites were used to relying on the priests, who were mediators between the

Israelites and God. It was the priests who offered sacrifices for sins and who entered into God's presence in the Most Holy Place. But because Jesus died on the cross, he opened access to God so that those who believe in him can communicate directly with him (Hebrews 10:19). The way is open to God the Father because Jesus has placed us in right standing with him. That is why prayer is so effective. The work of Jesus on the cross backs it up.

Do you appreciate the true power of prayer in your marriage? Do you imagine yourself entering God's presence when you pray? Thank Jesus today for opening the way to God the Father.

PRAYING GOD'S PROMISE

Dear Jesus, you promise that anyone who believes in you will do even greater works than you performed on this earth. We believe in you. We rely on you for our strength and hope. Work your will through us in mighty and awesome ways. You promise that we can ask anything in your name and you will do it. Make our meditations and thoughts, our requests and prayers pleasing to you. We're praying to God the Father in your name.

GOD'S PROMISE TO YOU

- God will empower you to do great works in his name.
- Jesus has opened your way to God the Father.

THE PROMISE
GOD OFFERS ETERNAL HOPE

May our Lord Jesus Christ and God our Father, who loved us and in his special favor gave us everlasting comfort and good hope, comfort your hearts and give you strength in every good thing you do and say.   2 Thessalonians 2:16-17

O N E of the worst feelings a person can have is a sense of hopelessness. Have you ever experienced it? When we have those feelings, we can't see how anything will ever change for the better. We can't see a light at the end of the tunnel. Sometimes the situation changes, and we begin to feel better. But we have no assurance that it won't get difficult and "hopeless" again. That's a horrible feeling.

When the apostle Paul speaks about hope, he's speaking about an eternal hope, one that has nothing to do with our circumstances at the moment. He's talking about a hope that God gives us, one that no one and nothing can take away from us. People who don't know Jesus as their Savior don't have this hope, and sometimes there are outward signs of their inner hopelessness. Some pursue temporary pleasure through climbing the career ladder and acquiring wealth. Some lead destructive lifestyles, abusing alcohol and drugs. If you are a Christian, your life and marriage are built on your hope in God, not on yourself, and the hope that God gives will never disappoint you.

He loves you, and he will see you through any situation, no matter how difficult or hopeless it might seem. The Bible promises that he will comfort you when you need comfort (Psalm 119:76) and he will give you strength to endure difficulties and to continue to do what is good (Ephesians 3:16). Find your hope in God, and ask him to give you his comfort and strength.

PRAYING GOD'S PROMISE

Dear Jesus, you love us so much that you show special favor to us in giving your everlasting comfort and good hope. Thank you for loving us so much. Help me to focus my life on the good hope you have given us. Strengthen me to stand firm in your truth and not be swayed by circumstances. Your Word promises that you will comfort our hearts and give us strength to do every good thing. We want to do good things in your name. Give us strength, and empower us to do that.

GOD'S PROMISE TO YOU

- God gives his people everlasting comfort and good hope.
- He can comfort your heart.
- He will strengthen you.

THE PROMISE
GOD GRANTS ETERNAL TREASURES

[Jesus said,] "Don't store up treasures here on earth, where they can be eaten by moths and get rusty, and where thieves break in and steal. Store your treasures in heaven, where they will never become moth-eaten or rusty and where they will be safe from thieves. Wherever your treasure is, there your heart and thoughts will also be. . . . No one can serve two masters. For you will hate one and love the other, or be devoted to one and despise the other. You cannot serve both God and money."

Matthew 6:19-21, 24

IT's natural for us to want to pour our energy and resources into what's significant; that is, things that will last. Have you ever had the experience of seeing something in which you invested lots of time and energy fail miserably? It's not a good feeling to know that those hours were wasted. Financial investments that fail are even more disappointing.

In today's passage Jesus encourages us to make an investment that makes sense, an investment that cannot lose. He invites us to invest our lives in things that are eternal, to store our treasures in heaven. How do we do that? Jesus gives us a hint when he says, "Wherever your treasure is, there your hearts and thoughts will also be." Whatever you spend the most time thinking about is where your treasure is. If it's your checking account or your stock portfolio, your treasure is in this world. If it's Christ and his kingdom, your investment is an eternal one.

Only when you fix your thoughts on what is unseen, on Jesus and his will for your lives, can you be confident in your investment, because that investment will last forever (2 Corinthians 4:18). Think about God's promise to give eternal treasure to those who set their hearts and thoughts on heaven. Then ask God to help you and your spouse to serve him alone and to seek his kingdom first (Matthew 6:33).

PRAYING GOD'S PROMISE

Dear Jesus, you promise that treasures stored in heaven will never disappear. We want to know that our investments are eternal. Help us to serve you with an undivided heart. Your Word promises that if we turn our hearts and thoughts toward you and your Word, you will be with us and we will store up lasting treasures. Today we fix our hearts and thoughts on you, Jesus. We want the energies we invest in our marriage to revolve around you.

GOD'S PROMISE TO YOU
- God will give his people treasures that last forever.

THE PROMISE
GOD DEFENDS US

W ho but God goes up to heaven and comes back down? W ho holds the wind in his fists? W ho wraps up the oceans in his cloak? W ho has created the whole wide world? W hat is his name—and his son's name? Tell me if you know! Every word of God proves true. He defends all who come to him for protection. Do not add to his words, or he may rebuke you, and you will be found a liar.   Proverbs 30:4-6

M A N Y of the promises in the Bible have two sides. We read that God will defend and protect those who follow him (1 Peter 1:5). But the Bible also speaks about God's abandoning those who abandon him and his ways (Ezra 8:22). God's wonderful promises to his people quickly turn into a curse on those who don't respond to God (Proverbs 3:33).

Today's passage demonstrates this. For those who are careful to follow God's Word, the promise that every word will prove true is comforting and uplifting. We can be confident that God's promise to rescue us from our sins and defend us will come true. But for those who add to God's word or ignore it, this promise is a threat. God will rebuke those who add to his words. He will punish those who ignore his offer of salvation. Being able to find comfort in God's promises is one of the joys God's people have. No matter how precarious or desperate our situation, we can know confidently that God is with us. Day after day he is guiding us to our eternal home. Every one of God's words will one day come true. Ask God to impress that promise on both you and your spouse and to give you great confidence in the One who made it so that you and your spouse are able to face whatever comes your way.

PRAYING GOD'S PROMISE

Dear God, Scripture promises that every one of your words will come true because you are the all-powerful Creator of the cosmos. We worship you. Only you can hold the wind in your fist. Only you wrap the oceans in your cloak. And only your words will come true. Help us to understand your words and apply them to our lives. We call on you to protect our marriage and our home. Defend us from the things that can destroy us. Help us to stand for you.

GOD'S PROMISE TO YOU

- All of God's words will come true.
- God will defend you if you call on him.

THE PROMISE
GOD BLESSES THE PURE OF HEART

[Jesus said,] "God blesses those who realize their need for him, for the Kingdom of Heaven is given to them. . . . God blesses those who are gentle and lowly, for the whole earth will belong to them. God blesses those who are hungry and thirsty for justice, for they will receive it in full. God blesses those who are merciful, for they will be shown mercy. God blesses those whose hearts are pure, for they will see God."   Matthew 5:3-8

GOD'S greatest promises are for those who, measured by the world's standards, don't appear to be blessed at all. Jesus clearly states that God blesses the poor (Luke 6:20), those who realize their need for God, those who mourn, and those who are gentle and lowly. The Israelites who heard Jesus say these things would have been just as surprised as we are by this list of people God will bless. The rich and powerful certainly appear to be enjoying God's blessings. We naturally think of those who are honored—not those who are lowly—as receiving God's blessing. Yet God's wisdom is higher than human wisdom (1 Corinthians 3:18-20). God doesn't judge by appearances. He searches the heart (Proverbs 17:3). If you want God's blessing, you need to understand God's perspective and ask him to align your life to his will.

You can learn what God desires by studying the Bible and

asking God to prepare your heart to understand and accept his truth. You can do that by doing what Jesus says in this passage: "realize [your] need for him." When you humble yourself before God and ask him to teach you, you become "lowly" before him.

Pray today that you and your spouse will encourage each other to search out God's wisdom in the Bible, and ask God to make you the kind of people he can bless.

PRAYING GOD'S PROMISE

Dear Jesus, you bless those who realize their need for you and those who are gentle and lowly. We acknowledge our need for you. We humble ourselves before you. We believe in you. Include us in your kingdom and bless us, just as your Word promises. You promise to bless those who are merciful and pure and who hunger and thirst for justice. Help us to show mercy to each other and to work for what is right and just. Purify our hearts and grant us your blessings.

GOD'S PROMISE TO YOU

- God will bless you when you acknowledge your need for him.
- He blesses those who show mercy to others and work for justice.
- He blesses those whose hearts are pure.

THE PROMISE
GOD WORKS FOR US

When you came down long ago, you did awesome things beyond our highest expectations. And oh, how the mountains quaked! For since the world began, no ear has heard, and no eye has seen a God like you, who works for those who wait for him! You welcome those who cheerfully do good, who follow godly ways. . . . Lord, you are our Father. We are the clay, and you are the potter. We are all formed by your hand.

Isaiah 64:3-5, 8

T HE prophet Isaiah originally gave these promises to the Israelites. Their ancestors had seen God's mighty and awesome acts firsthand. The mountains had quaked when God appeared to the Israelites at Mount Sinai (Exodus 19:18-19). The sea had parted when God rescued them from their Egyptian taskmasters (Exodus 14:21-22). But the Israelites of Isaiah's day had not experienced God's working in powerful ways because they had abandoned the true God for false gods. They had sought direction from idols instead of from the living God.

Even though many Israelites had abandoned God, however, some still waited on him. They still looked to God to protect them. These were the people to whom Isaiah gave these promises. God would reward them and vindicate them because of their faithfulness to him. God would again act in mighty ways, just as he had in the past.

At one time or another, most believers experience times when they wonder whether living for God is really worth it. Those who ignore God appear to be prospering, so why wait on God? Isaiah gives us the answer. One day God will act, and at that time our patience will be rewarded (James 5:7-8). God himself will welcome those who consistently and cheerfully follow him. Ask God to give you the patience and endurance to wait on him. He has said that "those who wait on the Lord will find new strength" (Isaiah 40:31). Take him at his word.

PRAYING GOD'S PROMISE

Dear God, your Word promises that you work for those who wait on you. We're quieting our hearts before you, oh God, and we wait on you to act in your time and in your way. We can't even imagine what good things you're preparing for us. We have read that you welcome those who cheerfully do good, those who follow godly ways. Help us to do good with cheerful hearts. We know we are formed by your hand, and we want to enjoy your welcome because we have followed your godly ways.

GOD'S PROMISE TO YOU

- God will work for you if you wait on him.
- He will welcome you if you continue to do good cheerfully.

THE PROMISE
GOD WILL AVENGE WRONGDOING

Dear friends, never avenge yourselves. Leave that to God. For it is written, "I will take vengeance; I will repay those who deserve it," says the Lord. Instead, do what the Scriptures say: "If your enemies are hungry, feed them. If they are thirsty, give them something to drink, and they will be ashamed of what they have done to you." Don't let evil get the best of you, but conquer evil by doing good.   Romans 12:19-21

O U R natural instinct is to strike back at those who hurt us. If someone accuses us, we tend to accuse that person and question his motives. If people attack our character, we look for an opportunity to point out their character flaws. The Bible tells us to restrain this impulse. Paybacks will only prompt more paybacks. Evil will only reproduce evil. We're supposed to demonstrate Christ's love to our enemies (Matthew 5:44). We're to find ways to do good to them. If they're in need of food, we should provide it. Even if they don't need anything, we can find ways to express goodwill through gifts. The Bible promises that in the end, good will conquer evil (Romans 12:21) and truth will win out over falsehood (Proverbs 12:19).

According to the Scriptures, the end never justifies the means. We can't create a good situation through lies or deceit or by treating our enemies badly. Goodness comes only from doing good. No matter what situation we find ourselves in, we need to judge our actions by the standard of God's Word and compare what we do to Christ's example.

Today as you pray, commit the wrongs that you have experienced to God. Trust him to judge the situation rightly. Then ask for the strength to show Christlike love to those who have hurt you. You can be assured that your willingness and determination to do good will bear fruit.

PRAYING GOD'S PROMISE

Dear God, your Word promises that you will avenge; you will repay those who deserve it. Here are the ways we have been wronged. We give these offenses to you. We trust you to restore justice to this situation. Help us to find ways to conquer evil by doing good to those who are against us. May our good actions conquer evil, as the Bible has promised.

GOD'S PROMISE TO YOU

- God will take vengeance on those who deserve it.
- Good will conquer evil.

THE PROMISE
THOSE WHO ARE PURE MAY ENTER
GOD'S PRESENCE

Who may climb the mountain of the Lord? Who may stand in his holy place? Only those whose hands and hearts are pure, who do not worship idols and never tell lies. They will receive the Lord's blessing and have right standing with God their savior. They alone may enter God's presence and worship the God of Israel.   Psalm 24:3-6

T HE miracle of prayer is that God, the holy Creator of the universe, allows us into his presence. God welcomes us because of what Jesus has done for us. We can enter God's presence because the blood of Jesus has cleansed our hands and hearts and given us right standing with God (Hebrews 10:22). All of the promises related to prayer depend on this amazing truth. Because of what Jesus has done, we can express our needs to God and be confident that he will answer. In fact, God will do more than answer. The Bible promises that God will bless us.

Before you pray, meditate on what it means to you to have the privilege of coming into God's presence in prayer. Then go ahead and confidently enter God's presence with praise and worship. Thank God for providing salvation through his Son and for listening to your requests.

PRAYING GOD'S PROMISE

Dear God, you bless those whose hands and hearts are pure, and you welcome them into your presence. Cleanse our hands and hearts. Make our marriage and our home pure. Help us to refrain from any kind of deceit so that you will shower your blessings on us. Only those who have been given right standing with you through Christ are able to enter your presence to worship you. Thank you for the right standing you have given us, and thank you, oh God, for listening to our prayers.

GOD'S PROMISE TO YOU

- God blesses those whose hearts and hands are pure.
- He welcomes those who are pure and truthful into his presence.

THE PROMISE
GOD LOVES US UNFAILINGLY

O Lord, you are so good, so ready to forgive, so full of unfailing love for all who ask your aid. Listen closely to my prayer, O Lord; hear my urgent cry. I will call to you whenever trouble strikes, and you will answer me. . . . But you, O Lord, are a merciful and gracious God, slow to get angry, full of unfailing love and truth. Look down and have mercy on me. Give strength to your servant; yes, save me, for I am your servant.

Psalm 86:5-7, 15-16

WHERE is God when trouble strikes? Where is God when everyone comes home at the end of the day disappointed and discouraged? Where is God when life seems to be going terribly wrong? The Bible promises that he's with us (Psalm 16:8), listening to our prayers, answering our calls for help. He wants to give us enough strength to get through our most difficult day.

Too often, when trouble strikes, we find ourselves desperately trying to save ourselves. We get busy trying to dig ourselves out of trouble. The Bible encourages us to stop working with such desperation and quiet our souls before God. It instructs us to commit our troubles and problems to him and ask for the wisdom and strength to continue (Psalm 40:12-13). The most effective thing we can do during difficult times is to call on God for help. He is powerful enough to handle any problem. He is

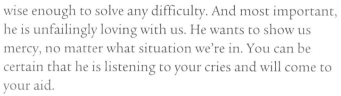

wise enough to solve any difficulty. And most important, he is unfailingly loving with us. He wants to show us mercy, no matter what situation we're in. You can be certain that he is listening to your cries and will come to your aid.

Take the problems and difficulties and disappointments you're experiencing today to God. Call on him for help, and rest in his promise to listen to your cries.

PRAYING GOD'S PROMISE

Dear God, your Word promises that you are ready to forgive us, that you will listen to our prayers and hear our cries. We call on you today, asking for your aid. Listen to our prayers. Show us your unfailing love. The Bible promises that you will answer us when we call on you. You are merciful and gracious to us, full of unfailing love for us. Be merciful to us. Give us strength that will see us through our troubles. Rescue us, for we want to serve you.

GOD'S PROMISE TO YOU

- God will answer you when you call on him.
- He will listen to your prayers.
- He shows mercy and unfailing love to his servants.

THE PROMISE
GOD STRENGTHENS US

Hanani the seer came to King Asa and told him, "Because you have put your trust in the king of Aram instead of in the Lord your God, you missed your chance to destroy the army of the king of Aram. Don't you remember what happened to the Ethiopians and Libyans and their vast army, with all of their chariots and horsemen ? At that time you relied on the Lord, and he handed them all over to you. The eyes of the Lord search the whole earth in order to strengthen those whose hearts are fully committed to him."   2 Chronicles 16:7-9

E ARLY in Asa's reign, an army of a million men from Ethiopia invaded Judah. Asa's army was outnumbered, yet he didn't give up. He brought his predicament to God in prayer: "O Lord, no one but you can help the powerless against the mighty! Help us, O Lord our God, for we trust in you alone" (2 Chronicles 14:11). The Bible says that God rescues those who call on him in times of trouble (Psalm 91:14-15). God backed up this promise for Asa when he cried out to God. We can be assured that God will strengthen us in our day of trouble. God loves to deliver those who rely on him for strength (Psalm 91:1-2).

When the king of Israel attacked King Asa in Judah later in Asa's reign, Asa forgot the lessons he learned in his youth. Instead of turning to God for help as he had done in the past, he turned to a pagan king—King Ben-Hadad of Aram—for help. God certainly knew King Asa needed help, but he wasn't going to share the glory of a victory over the invaders with a pagan king. He sent the seer Hanani to King Asa with a message: *God would have helped you if only you had asked. God is searching the earth for those whose hearts are fully committed to him.* Pray today that the hearts of you and your spouse will always be fully committed to God. Remind God of his promises to come to the aid of those who call on him.

PRAYING GOD'S PROMISE

Dear Lord, your Word promises that if we rely on you when we're experiencing danger and trouble, you will strengthen us. We're relying on you, oh God, to strengthen our marriage and to deliver us from danger. Your Word promises that you will strengthen those whose hearts are fully committed to you. We commit our hearts to you. Strengthen us for the troubles we will face, and cause our marriage to endure as we call upon you.

GOD'S PROMISE TO YOU

● God will strengthen you when you are fully committed to him.

THE PROMISE
GOD MAKES US HIS OWN

What harmony can there be between Christ and the Devil?
How can a believer be a partner with an unbeliever? And
what union can there be between God's temple and idols? For
we are the temple of the living God. As God said: "I will live
in them and walk among them. I will be their God, and they
will be my people. Therefore, come out from them and separate
yourselves from them, says the Lord. Don't touch their filthy
things, and I will welcome you. And I will be your Father, and
you will be my sons and daughters, says the Lord Almighty."

2 Corinthians 6:15-18

SPRING cleaning is always an adventure. You climb into corners
of your home that you haven't touched in a long time. You
open boxes that have been in the attic or basement for months.
Dust flies everywhere. In some ways it's amazing how much dirt
we live with. Spring cleaning exposes those dark, dirty corners
to the light—and to Spic and Span.

God commands us to do that same thing with our lives. They
have to be absolutely clean because the holy God lives among
us—and he requires holy living (1 Peter 1:16). Sometimes, as
before we begin spring cleaning, we don't even realize that we're
living in filth. But God sees with crystal clarity the dirt and sin
we've allowed to build up in our lives. He wants us to commit

those dirty parts to him for his cleansing. He is our Father, and we should represent him in the best possible way.

Carve out some time this week with your spouse to commit your marriage and home to God. Walk through your home, and then figuratively walk through your life, asking God to point out the sins that need attention.

PRAYING GOD'S PROMISE

Dear God, you promise that you will live among us and make us your people. You promise to welcome us when we separate ourselves from the filth of sin. We want to keep ourselves from anyone or anything that causes us to sin. Live among us, as you have promised in your Word. Welcome us as your people. Help us to recognize filth in our home and our marriage and to get rid of it. Make us your genuine sons and daughters, as you have promised.

GOD'S PROMISE TO YOU

- God will live among his people.
- He will welcome you if you separate yourself from sin.
- He will make you his child.

THE PROMISE
GOD WORKS OUT HIS PLAN

The Lord will work out his plans for my life—for your faithful love, O Lord, endures forever.   Psalm 138: 8

W HETHER you're a long-term planner or a person who's more spontaneous, you probably have plans or dreams for yourself. In your mind's eye you can see where you want to be. God also has a plan for you and for your marriage. But God's plan isn't a fuzzy idea of what your future could bring. He has known you from your birth (Psalm 71:6), and he already knows what will happen (Romans 8:28-30). He knows what circumstances and people he will allow into your life and what things he will block from your home (1 Corinthians 10:13).

God knows what he wants to accomplish through you and through your marriage (Psalm 33:11). He has created everything for his purposes, and he has called you to live a pure life (1 Thessalonians 4:7). Spend some time praying that God will fulfill his purpose in your marriage. Ask him to make you and your spouse open to receiving and obeying his will.

PRAYING GOD'S PROMISE

Dear Lord, your Word promises that you will answer us when we pray to you, that you will encourage us by giving us strength. Give us the strength we need, as you have promised. Encourage us in the work you have given us to do. We trust that you will work out the plans for our life together. You promise to preserve us when we're surrounded by troubles. Thank you for loving us enough to have a plan for our marriage. Help us to bend to your will—to willingly cooperate and participate as you work out your plan for our home.

GOD'S PROMISE TO YOU

- God will work out his plans for your life.
- His faithful love lasts forever.

THE PROMISE
GOD INSPIRES HAPPINESS IN THOSE
WHO FEAR HIM

Happy are those who fear the Lord. Yes, happy are those who delight in doing what he commands. Their children will be successful everywhere; an entire generation of godly people will be blessed. They themselves will be wealthy, and their good deeds will never be forgotten.   Psalm 112:1-3

IF our culture were to reword the verses of this psalm, we may be reading the following "proverbs": Happy are those who find good jobs. Happy are those who enjoy fame. Happy are those who have free time to spend on entertainment.

God's Word, however, tells us to look elsewhere for happiness. True happiness isn't found in security and wealth, it's found in fearing and respecting God. Genuine joy isn't found in owning and enjoying the latest and best thing. It's found in doing what God commands. It is when we humble ourselves before God and endeavor to follow him alone that we can experience the joy of living in line with our Creator's original intention. We can live a balanced life, one that is in sync with the way God created us. Not only will we be happy when we respect God's will for our lives, but our marriages and homes will know God's blessing as well. The good deeds we do in God's name won't be forgotten. Our efforts will fit into God's eternal purposes. And our work will never be futile because it will bear everlasting fruit (John 15:1-5).

PRAYING GOD'S PROMISE

Dear God, your Word promises that those who fear and respect you will be happy. We respect your Word. We want to please you and live according to your decrees. Grant us genuine joy and happiness as we do that. Those who delight in obeying your commands will be happy. Their good deeds won't be forgotten. Help us to delight in following you. Help us to do good so that you will bless our marriage with happiness.

GOD'S PROMISE TO YOU

- Fearing and obeying God's commands brings happiness.
- Your good deeds won't be forgotten.

THE PROMISE
GOD GIVES POWER TO THE WEARY

How can you say the Lord does not see your troubles? How
can you say God refuses to hear your case? Have you never
heard or understood? Don't you know that the Lord is the
everlasting God, the Creator of all the earth? He never grows
faint or weary. No one can measure the depths of his understanding. He gives power to those who are tired and worn out;
he offers strength to the weak. Even youths will become
exhausted, and young men will give up. But those who wait on
the Lord will find new strength. They will fly high on wings
like eagles. They will run and not grow weary. They will walk
and not faint.   Isaiah 40:27-31

IF we're not careful, our frantic, overpacked days can distort our
view of reality. Like a driver racing through the dark, we peer
forward, straining to see what's ahead. Sometimes we're moving
so fast that it's impossible for us to react to surprises that may
be in the road. Often the pace of our lives makes small problems seem large. Branches in the road become roadblocks.

The prophet Isaiah asks us the same thing he asked the Israelites of his day: "Have you never heard or understood?" Don't
you understand that God is bigger than your problems and
agenda? Slow down to look away from the road and up to the
heavens. God is the Creator of the stars in the sky and the road

ahead. He sees what you're doing, the troubles you're experiencing, and the difficulties that await you in the future. He is all-powerful and all-wise.

We have the same invitation that the Israelites of Isaiah's day had: to call on the everlasting God, for he gives strength to the weak and power to those who are weary (2 Corinthians 12:9-10). Those who wait on God to act in his time and his way will find renewed strength. As you pray, ask God to help you and your spouse to slow down, to consider who God is, and to remember that he is able to give you power when you are weary. Then give your problems to God, and wait patiently for him to give you the strength you both need.

PRAYING GOD'S PROMISE

Dear God, the Scriptures promise that you give power to the tired and strength to the weak. We acknowledge that as the Creator of the earth your power is limitless. We also acknowledge that as your creatures we are tired and weak. Give us your power, as your Word promises. We know that you see and understand all of our troubles and that you hear our prayers. We wait on you to act. Provide renewed strength and hope to us in our marriage.

GOD'S PROMISE TO YOU

- God gives power to those who are tired and worn out.
- He will give you renewed strength as you wait for him to act.

THE PROMISE
GOD MAKES HIS PEOPLE NEW

God saved you by his special favor when you believed. And you can't take credit for this; it is a gift from God. Salvation is not a reward for the good things we have done, so none of us can boast about it. For we are God's masterpiece. He has created us anew in Christ Jesus, so that we can do the good things he planned for us long ago.

Ephesians 2:8-10

WHAT do you boast about? Your home? Your children? Your abilities or your career? If you are a Christian, there isn't any room for boasting. Everything you have in this life is a gift from God, and so is the life you will spend with him in eternity. You can't do anything to earn your salvation or eternal life. God alone saved you from your sins. In fact, you were still spiritually dead—unable to help yourself—when he saved you. God is the One who brought you to life because of what Jesus did for you on the cross (1 John 4:9-10). So anything you accomplish, anything you may do for good, is the result of God's power at work in you. The good you do is a testimony to how great and good God is.

Yes, today's passage calls you a "masterpiece," but that isn't anything to brag about either. The *Mona Lisa* is a masterpiece, but the paint and canvas can't take any credit for what it became. It is only a reflection of the painter's artistry. You are

God's masterpiece. Any glory you may attain reflects the skill and wisdom of your maker.

Boasting is a very good way to destroy your marriage because those who boast are seeking to exalt themselves over others—and too often a husband or wife is the first one who is demeaned when a spouse boasts.

Think through your life and your marriage. In what ways can you identify God working to make you and your spouse into masterpieces? How has God shown his mercy and special favor on your home? Find ways today to thank God for his special work in your marriage.

PRAYING GOD'S PROMISE

Dear God, you are rich in mercy. You loved us so much that you saved us out of your special favor and made us one with Jesus. Thank you for loving us so deeply. Nothing we do on our own could ever have earned your favor and gained us salvation. We are your masterpieces. You created us anew in Jesus, so we can do the good things you planned for us to do. We want to live according to your good plan for us so that our lives and our marriages are clear reflections of your goodness and your power to make us new.

GOD'S PROMISE TO YOU

- God saves you because of his special favor.
- He is making you into a masterpiece that reflects his power.

THE PROMISE
GOD USES THE PURE

Expensive utensils are used for special occasions, and the cheap ones are for everyday use. If you keep yourself pure, you will be a utensil God can use for his purpose. Your life will be clean, and you will be ready for the Master to use you for every good work.   2 Timothy 2:20-21

S OLDIERS in the army spend much time cleaning their equipment—especially their rifles. No one wants a dirty rifle to jam at a critical moment on the battlefield. The same thing happens when a chef prepares a kitchen for an upcoming banquet. He wants the kitchen clean and ready for him to use. All of his cooking utensils are clean before he starts. If a pot is dirty, he won't use it.

The same is true for the Christian life. When our lives are clean and pure, they're ready for God to use for his good purposes. Let us do everything we can to make our lives and marriages clean utensils ready for the Master's use. That's what the apostle Paul encouraged Timothy to be in today's verses. How do we make our lives pure? First, we can ask God to cleanse our hearts and home (1 John 1:9). Second, we can ask him to help us guard against evil entering our home. Third, we can ask him to help us run from anything that distracts us from pursuing him.

Spend time in prayer today asking God to help you identify impurity in your home and in your life. Then ask him to cleanse you and your home so you will be clean utensils that God can use.

PRAYING GOD'S PROMISE

Dear God, the Bible says that your truth stands firm like a foundation stone. You know those who belong to you, and they will turn away from evil. We are building our marriage around your truth because we know it's a firm foundation. Claim us, oh God, as your people so that we can live holy lives. Help us to lead pure lives, so we are ready when you want to use us. We want our marriage, our home—our very lives—to be tools you can use to accomplish your good purposes.

GOD'S PROMISE TO YOU

- When you keep yourself pure, God will use you to accomplish his purpose.

THE PROMISE
GOD JOINED US TOGETHER

"Haven't you read the Scriptures?" Jesus replied. "They record that from the beginning 'God made them male and female.' And he said, 'This explains why a man leaves his father and mother and is joined to his wife, and the two are united into one.' Since they are no longer two but one, let no one separate them, for God has joined them together."   Matthew 19:4-6

WEDDINGS are grand occasions. We decorate churches with bright flower arrangements. We make finger sandwiches and cakes. Moms and dads, aunts and uncles, grandmothers and grandfathers all come in their best clothes. Friends and family gather to watch a couple declare their love and commitment to each other. Among the witnesses is God himself. At every Christian wedding God is present, celebrating the couple's love for each other. Jesus describes God himself as joining the couple together, making the new husband and wife one.

Do you remember who came to your wedding? Have you ever meditated on the thought that God himself was there with both of you on that day? When the preacher declared you husband and wife, God himself united both of you into one. In today's passage Jesus issues a challenge: "Let no one separate them, for God has joined them together." God is pleased when he sees a husband and wife remaining faithful to each other, loving each other year after year. Pray for your marriage today. Ask God to strengthen and support the union he created when you and your spouse married. Ask him to be at the center of your marriage just as he was at the center of your wedding.

PRAYING GOD'S PROMISE
Dear Lord, you made us for each other—male and female. Thank you for creating the marriage union in the beginning. When we entered into marriage, you made us one. Thank you for creating us for each other. Help us to identify and get rid of anything that may separate us or weaken our commitment to each other. Strengthen and protect our union.

GOD'S PROMISE TO YOU
- God unites into one those who enter into marriage.
- He wants spouses to stay committed to each other.

THE PROMISE
JESUS KNOWS OUR WEAKNESSES

We have a great High Priest who has gone to heaven, Jesus
the Son of God. Let us cling to him and never stop trusting
him. This High Priest of ours understands our weaknesses, for
he faced all of the same temptations we do, yet he did not sin.
So let us come boldly to the throne of our gracious God. There
we will receive his mercy, and we will find grace to help us
when we need it.   Hebrews 4:14-16

T HE stark light of God's Word exposes the truth about our
lives—our innermost thoughts and desires, everything we have
said and done. Under its penetrating examination, none of us
can appear pure. We all have the ugly stain of sin. But those
who believe in Jesus have a perfect high priest in Jesus Christ
himself, who intercedes on their behalf. Yes, it's true. None of
us can hide anything from God, who sees all. Our sympathetic
High Priest knows and understands our weaknesses. He knows
how difficult it is to resist temptation because he was tempted
in the same way we are, but he didn't sin. It's because of our
perfect High Priest that we can boldly enter God's throne room
in prayer. Today's verses promise that when we do, we will
receive the mercy and grace we need. Today as you pray, thank
Jesus for being your sympathetic high priest, and ask him to
intercede for you and your spouse today. His grace is always
available to you when you need it.

PRAYING GOD'S PROMISE

Dear God, your Word tells us that because of what Jesus, our High Priest, has done, we can enter your throne room with confidence, knowing that you will give us the mercy and grace that we need. Thank you for that privilege. Cleanse our innermost thoughts and desires so that you will welcome us into your presence when we pray. The Bible tells us that Jesus understands our weaknesses and knows the temptations we face. Thank you for the comfort of knowing that our High Priest is understanding and sympathetic. We cling to you, Jesus, and to your grace and mercy.

GOD'S PROMISE TO YOU

- God shows mercy to those who have Jesus as their High Priest.
- He will give you his grace when you ask him for it.
- Jesus understands your weakness and the temptations you face.

THE PROMISE
GOD PROMISES JOY THAT WILL LAST FOREVER

Though our bodies are dying, our spirits are being renewed every day. For our present troubles are quite small and won't last very long. Yet they produce for us an immeasurably great glory that will last forever! So we don't look at the troubles we can see right now; rather, we look forward to what we have not yet seen. For the troubles we see will soon be over, but the joys to come will last forever.   2 Corinthians 4:16-18

O N E reason that we study God's Word and pray is to correct our perspective on life. Believers and unbelievers often have the same experiences. God allows the rain to replenish the land of the godly and ungodly alike (Matthew 5:45). Both unbelievers and believers enjoy God's good gifts to this earth—the seasons, the food, warm sunny days, and cool nights. Often believers and unbelievers experience the same types of troubles, conflicts, and financial stresses. But believers should have a fundamentally different perspective on them

Their responses to the vicissitudes of life should be different from the reactions of their unbelieving friends and neighbors. Believers should follow a different compass—God's truth—throughout life. In today's verses the apostle Paul demonstrated to the Corinthians that he was careful to view his present troubles with an eternal perspective. He measured the suffering he was going through against the eternal joy and immeasurable glory God will allow him to experience in heaven. We need to do the same.

Spend some time meditating on what it will be like to live harmoniously with our loving Creator in heaven. Ask God to give you an idea of what you can look forward to in heaven, and then work on developing a more eternal perspective.

PRAYING GOD'S PROMISE

Dear God, although our bodies are slowly declining, we have your promise that you will raise us to life again. We see our bodies age and change, but you renew our spirits every day. Your Word promises that our present troubles will soon be over and we will experience a joy that will last forever. We give you our troubles and ask you to help us see them from the perspective of eternity. We may have sorrows in this life, but our joy in heaven will last forever.

GOD'S PROMISE TO YOU

- Those who believe in Jesus will be raised to eternal life.
- God will give believers a joy that lasts forever.

THE PROMISE
GOD REMOVES OUR GUILT

When I refused to confess my sin, I was weak and miserable, and I groaned all day long. Day and night your hand of discipline was heavy on me. My strength evaporated like water in the summer heat. . . . I confessed all my sins to you and stopped trying to hide them. I said to myself, "I will confess my rebellion to the Lord." And you forgave me! All my guilt is gone.   Psalm 32:3-5

CHILDREN can rarely hide their guilt. It's written all over their faces when they do something wrong. They even refuse to look at their parents' faces because they know their parents will see the guilty look in their children's eyes. Adults are much better at hiding guilt. But the fact is, guilt can be debilitating, and a heavy conscience can cripple us. The sin we bury deep inside our souls eats away at us. Our consciences remind us again and again that we've done wrong.

Eventually our guilt can begin to affect our close relationships. We may lash out at our spouses for no reason, or we may withdraw. David, the writer of today's verses, experienced this. When he refused to confess his sin, he became "weak" and "miserable," groaning all day long. His strength left him because his sin weighed heavily on him. But when he decided to be honest with God, when he confessed his sin, God lifted

David's heavy burden of guilt. Then David could shout: "Oh, what joy for those whose rebellion has been forgiven" (Psalm 32:1). Confess your sins to God today. Ask him to forgive you. He will free you from the burden of any guilt you may have.

PRAYING GOD'S PROMISE

Dear God, your Word promises that you will forgive those who confess their sins to you. You will clear our record of sin if we admit our rebellious attitudes and actions. We confess our sins to you. We admit our rebellion. Please forgive us. Help us to live honestly before you. Hiding our guilt from you only brings more heartache. Cleanse us from our guilt and restore us. Thank you for saving us from your judgment.

GOD'S PROMISE TO YOU

- God will forgive you and remove your guilt when you confess your sins to him.

THE PROMISE
GOD DOES NOT WANT US TO BE FEARFUL

God has not given us a spirit of fear and timidity, but of power, love, and self-discipline. So you must never be ashamed to tell others about our Lord.   2 Timothy 1:7-8

W HEN do you find yourself fearful or timid? During a piano recital or a play? When you're with people you don't know? Have you ever been timid about expressing your devotion to God? Most people feel timid at one time or another, but when it comes to telling others about God, the Bible encourages believers to be courageous and outspoken (1 Thessalonians 2:2). In today's verses the apostle Paul encouraged Timothy not to be fearful or timid—especially when it came to using the spiritual gifts God had given him. Paul pointed out to Timothy that God isn't a fearful or timid God. He is powerful and loving, and he gives us a spirit of love and power. That's why no matter what spiritual gift God has given you, you need to find opportunities to develop and use it (1 Peter 4:10-11). When you do, God will receive glory.

Spend time today praying about how you can use your spiritual gifts to bring glory to God. Encourage your spouse to use his or her spiritual gifts as well. Ask God to give you and your spouse opportunities to tell others how good and great he is.

PRAYING GOD'S PROMISE

Dear God, you have given each one of us a special gift. Help us to understand what abilities you have given us and how we can develop those abilities for your glory. You haven't given us a spirit of fear or timidity but of power, love, and self-discipline. We give you our fears. Help us to speak your words with power and love. Help us to live self-disciplined lives. Let us use our gifts to show others how wonderful you are.

GOD'S PROMISE TO YOU

- God gives each of his people a spiritual gift.
- He wants you to use your gift to reflect his glory to others.
- He gives you a spirit of power and love.

THE PROMISE
GOD GIVES US ONE HEART AND MIND

They will be my people, and I will be their God. And I will give them one heart and mind to worship me forever, for their own good and for the good of all their descendants. And I will make an everlasting covenant with them, promising not to stop doing good for them. I will put a desire in their hearts to worship me, and they will never leave me. I will rejoice in doing good to them and will faithfully and wholeheartedly replant them in this land.   Jeremiah 32:38-41

A F T E R predicting the fall of Jerusalem, the prophet Jeremiah gave the people of Judah this wonderful promise: God would one day give them new hearts and minds that would desire to worship him. He would make an everlasting covenant with his people, promising never to stop doing good to them. Although the people of Jeremiah's time were facing a frightening future with an army invading their land, they could look forward to a time when God would restore them (Jeremiah 32:37).

We are the beneficiaries of the promises Jeremiah spoke of so long ago. In today's passage Jeremiah describes the new covenant that Jesus established with his death on the cross (Hebrews 9:13-15). By offering himself as a sacrifice for our sins, Jesus reconciled us to God (1 Timothy 2:5-7). When we believe in Jesus, God makes us into new creations and implants the Holy

Spirit deep in our hearts. He is the One who creates in us the desire to worship God and follow him (Philippians 2:13). And because we are God's own children, he rejoices in doing good things for us. What a wonderful promise!

Pray this week that you and your spouse will be of one heart and mind in your desire to worship God and obey his ways. That is the best way to maintain unity in your home and marriage.

PRAYING GOD'S PROMISE

Dear God, you promise to make your people of one heart and mind in worshiping you. We want to worship you alone. Unite us in our desire to serve you. Keep us from wanting to wander away from you. You have made an everlasting covenant with your people, and you rejoice in doing good to us. Thank you for keeping your covenant. Help us to live for you.

GOD'S PROMISE TO YOU

- God gives his people one heart and mind to worship him forever.
- He has made an everlasting covenant with his people.
- He rejoices in doing good to you.

THE PROMISE
GOD IS NOT EASILY ANGERED

The Lord says, "Turn to me now, while there is time! Give me your hearts. Come with fasting, weeping, and mourning. Don't tear your clothing in your grief; instead, tear your hearts." Return to the Lord your God, for he is gracious and merciful. He is not easily angered. He is filled with kindness and is eager not to punish you.   Joel 2:12-13

I F you know anything about ancient mythology, you know that the false gods of ancient times were very fickle. The gods of Mount Olympus, for instance, could grow angry for no apparent reason, at least in the minds of the people who suffered the effects of the terrible wrath of these unpredictable gods.

Just like the people of ancient times, we may think that the living God is easily angered by what we do when in fact, just the opposite is true: He lovingly and patiently pursues his people to bring them back when they wander away and get lost (Ezekiel 34:12, 16).

God isn't easily angered. He graciously gives us time to turn from our evil ways. But God won't let sin go unpunished forever (Exodus 34:6-7). The prophet Joel said that on the Day of Judgment, God will appear in glory and power (Joel 2:10-11), to judge the world (Joel 3:12-14), and to save those who call on him (Joel 2:31-32). That is why Joel and the other prophets exhort their hearers to repent of their sins (Ezekiel 14:6). When that day comes, we will want to be following God, for only his perfect Son, Jesus, can save us from judgment (Romans 5:9-10).

Thank God today for being gracious and merciful and for being slow to become angry with you. Confess your sins to him, and ask him to restore spiritual health in your home.

PRAYING GOD'S PROMISE

Dear God, you promise to receive those who turn from their sins and turn to you. We are truly sorry for our sins, oh God. We give you our hearts and lives, and we ask you to receive us and to restore our relationship with you. Your Word promises that you are gracious and merciful to those who return to you. Thank you for not becoming angry with us. Your patience is so great. You are filled with kindness toward us. Thank you for showing mercy to us. Help us to live in a way that pleases you.

GOD'S PROMISE TO YOU

- God accepts those who give him their hearts.
- God will be gracious and merciful to you when you return to him.

THE PROMISE
JESUS CARRIED OUR SINS

It was our weaknesses he carried; it was our sorrows that weighed him down. . . . All of us have strayed away like sheep. We have left God's paths to follow our own. Yet the Lord laid on [Jesus] the guilt and sins of us all. . . . It was the Lord's good plan to crush him and fill him with grief. Yet when his life is made an offering for sin, he will have a multitude of children, many heirs.   Isaiah 53:4-6, 10

T HE greatest promise of all is that God saves all those who believe in him (John 3:16-18). All of us were on a path to eternal punishment until God reached out and saved us (Romans 5:6-8). The Bible says that we were all rebels against our Creator. We were like sheep that had strayed from their shepherd, when God sent his only Son to earth to die for us.

Although Jesus was completely perfect, he suffered and died for our sins (Hebrews 5:7-10). He carried our weakness. Our sorrows weighed him down. Our sins wounded and crushed him. All of this was part of God's wonderful plan for his people. What Jesus suffered fulfilled the many promises God had made concerning a Savior who would come into the world (Isaiah 62:11). God didn't shrink from fulfilling his promises even when it hurt him—even when he had to give up his innocent only Son to die a horrible and humiliating death.

The greatest promise in the entire Bible is God's promise to save those who believe in his Son (Romans 3:23-26). Ask God to impress this precious promise on your hearts and to help you live out your marriage from this day forward in gratitude for all that God has done for you.

PRAYING GOD'S PROMISE

Dear God, how can we thank you for all that Jesus has done for us? He was wounded because of our sins. He was beaten so that we might have peace. He was whipped so that we might be healed. We're sorry for all the sorrow we caused Jesus. But we are so thankful that by his death he gave us life. May we always live for you. May our home and our marriage be committed to sharing with others the good news of what Christ did when he carried our sins to the cross.

GOD'S PROMISE TO YOU

- God has placed your sin and guilt on his Son, Jesus.
- God will count you as righteous when you believe in Jesus.

SCRIPTURE INDEX

JON FARRAR is the acquisitions editor for Bibles and nonfiction for Tyndale House Publishers and is the author of *Looking Forward to Christmas: Family Devotions for the Season*. He is a graduate of Wheaton College, where he majored in history and theology. Jon and his wife, Isabel, live in West Chicago, Illinois, with their son, Ian. In his spare time Jon enjoys spending time with Isabel and sipping coffee at any place that has a view of Lake Michigan.

ABOUT THE AUTHOR

PRAYING GOD'S PROMISES SERIES